Escape From Democratic Kampuchea

**A Cambodian doctor's memoir of his grim
survival and harrowing escape from
Democratic Kampuchea**

Seiha Chea

Translated and Edited by
Oh Puay Fong

BALBOA.
PRESS

A DIVISION OF HAY HOUSE

Balboa Press books may be ordered through
booksellers or by contacting:

Balboa Press
A Division of Hay House
1663 Liberty Drive
Bloomington, IN 47403
www.balboapress.com
1 (877) 407-4847

Print information available on the last page.

ISBN: 978-1-5043-5964-1 (sc)
ISBN: 978-1-5043-5965-8 (e)

Balboa Press rev. date: 08/25/2016

Contents

For posterity

Preface

When I first read the Khmer book, *Escape from Democratic Kampuchea* by Dr. Chea Seiha, it struck me that his traumatic life experience during the Khmer Rouge regime holds many lessons for our young who are blessed to live in peace and prosperity. It is easy to overlook the importance of many things we take for granted when our lives are relatively rosy and sweet, such as our country's sovereignty or stability; personal liberties; filial piety and familial bonds; friendship; daily essentials such as food and water, or even soap; fluency in a different language; faith and religious freedom; hope, courage and determination in the face of adversity. What would we do if these were suddenly taken away from us?

Change being the only constant in life, it is imperative that we learn from the generations before us and consciously prevent or resist threats to our survival before these occur.

I also hope this memoir can inspire readers during their times of despondency: if Dr. Chea, who knew nothing about survival in the wild, could subsist alone in the forest for more than a fortnight without food or water but merely on faith and determination, many of our myriad problems come to appear surmountable in comparison. His fighting spirit is worth emulating and inculcating in our young to prepare them to meet life's challenges.

For Dr. Chea, putting his recollections on paper is necessarily cathartic, but what is commendable is that he chooses to give thanks despite his painful experience. Expressing gratitude to his birth and adopted countries, the Buddha (his religion), the Catholic priests who helped him, family, friends, anonymous strangers and even Mother Earth, he demonstrates clearly the interconnections that weave all of existence together. One interesting point to ponder: Gaia's bounty provides and sustains us, yet we are destroying forests and natural habitats at alarming rates. Are we sabotaging our own future?

Every language has its own peculiarities that endow it with color and flavor. Khmer is no different. The frequent use of alliterations, redundancies for emphasis and other literary devices may seem long-winded and awkward in English, but I have retained them to preserve the authenticity and essence of the original Khmer work and to allow Dr. Chea's voice to come through.

Some notes on my translation: at times I have discarded a one-to-one mapping of the Khmer alphabet to its commonly accepted English equivalent in favor of preserving the sound of a word while keeping it coherent in the target language. The Khmer language is largely phonetic, so my priority has been to retain the sound of a word, if sometimes at the expense of its conventional spelling. This makes more sense, as most young readers will have trouble articulating a word that starts with double consonants, followed by three vowels and ending with a silent consonant, for example. However, for words that have been anglicized and widely accepted, I have followed the conventional spelling.

The memoir is largely self-explanatory, although the events have been organized to fit into a book, so they are not presented in strict chronological order. In addition, I have inserted a few editorial comments when appropriate for readers unfamiliar with Cambodia's history, culture, beliefs, practices, geography, flora and fauna to provide glimpses into these. My rendition is therefore more accurately described as a transliteration, rather than a direct transcription. Consequently, I accept responsibility for all errors and omissions and welcome suggestions for improvement.

It is commonly assumed that the Khmer Rouge completely abolished medical care, as all educated professionals such as doctors were massacred. However, Dr. Chea's first-person account provides a historical record of how medical care was administered in Democratic Kampuchea. While Dr. Chea's recollection of events that happened more than thirty years ago is inevitably subject to memory lapses, his recollection remains an important contribution to the oral history of Cambodia's tragic past.

I am deeply honored to have worked on both the English and Chinese translations of this book, and thank Dr. Chea Seiha for giving me the opportunity.

I am also grateful to Ong Ling for the time and trouble taken to review the draft of the English manuscript, especially for her helpful comments; and to all my family and friends for their unwavering support.

The Curse of the Khmer Republic

By the end of 1974, the Khmer Republic led by Lon Nol was in rapid decline. It became increasingly clear that his Republican government was losing ground. As 1975 began, many of these Republicans fled the country with the illegal assets that they had accumulated from corruption while in office. In fact, soon after the 1970 *coup d'etat*, the newly-formed Khmer Republican government had splintered into various factions only interested in maximizing their personal gains from corruption. Internal strife and collusion were rife.

Senior military officials enriched themselves with the salaries of fictitious "ghost soldiers" that existed only in name on the payroll. They also sold military weapons and medical supplies to the Vietcong, the name of the communist revolutionary army of South Vietnam headed by Nguyen Huu Tho, and left the task of transporting these items to their junior staff. The

Vietcong forces had many camps along the eastern border of the Khmer Republic.

Before the 1970 *coup*, North Vietnamese forces were smuggling weapons and other supplies via the Ho Chi Minh Trail (through Cambodia) while the Chinese were doing the same via Sihanoukville Port. (The Cambodians took over such smuggling after the *coup*.)

After the 1970 *coup* deposing Samdech Sihanouk (the former king who passed away in Beijing on 15 October 2012 at 89 years old), the Vietcong seized the opportunity to attack the Khmer Republic forces, starting with their 27 March 1970 attack on the Chheu Khmau military base in Koh Thom. Their incursion subsequently expanded to other areas, reaching as far as the armor battalion at the old stadium in Phnom Penh before retreating to the lake named Boeng Kom Blaok in Kbal Thnal. These Vietcong soldiers wore photos of Samdech Norodom Sihanouk on their helmets or uniforms and declared that they had come to liberate the country to return Samdech to power. Such Vietcong offensives from 1970 to 1972 helped to pave the way for the Khmer Rouge. Without them, the Khmer Rouge could not have successfully captured the Khmer Republic so easily.

With the country in turbulence, the opportunists exploited the occasion to racketeer for their own selfish gains. They were not concerned that they were destroying the republic for money. They smuggled medicine, food, even gunpowder to the Vietcong and the Khmer Rouge forces. This smuggling helped the Khmer Rouge a great deal. When the Khmer Rouge came to power, these corrupt opportunists fled to Thailand. The Thai forces had heard of their misdeeds and completely expropriated their wealth before eventually sending them off to a third country. Those who did not flee in time received the same treatment from the Khmer Rouge, which confiscated all their wealth. When peace returned to the country, the craftiest ones who had managed to escape returned to buy themselves comfortable high positions in the government.

The Khmer Republic was doomed from the start, beginning with its 1970 *coup*. Its leaders did not have the right to decide. The Americans and South Vietnamese, whom the Khmer Republicans called "friendly allies," could do whatever they liked on Khmer soil, even killing Khmer people. Violent atrocities such as shooting the Khmer people, running tanks over them, carpet bombing, torture, rape and robberies took place without a whimper from the Khmer Republican leaders. They

3

did not protest when American forces dropped nearly three tons of bombs on Khmer soil and killed almost half a million people. Bombs turned half the sky east of the Mekong River yellow.

Besides the carpet bombing, there was yellow powder sprinkled from the skies. At that time, my house was at Kampong Dor Koh Krobei on the west bank of Takhmau district. In the mornings, I saw the yellow powder as it rained onto the cover of the big water jar outside my house. We did not know what it was. (Was it the Agent Orange used during the Vietnam War?) The Khmer Republican government was completely silent and took no action. The Americans and South Vietnamese liked the Khmer Republicans as they were "pro-American" and "pro-South Vietnamese." Moreover, they needed the Khmer Republicans to destroy the shelters of the North Vietnamese and to destroy the Ho Chi Minh Trail in Khmer territory.

Thanks to this friendly alliance, the Khmer Republicans occupied themselves with women, gambling and entertainment. A culture of flattery, rumors and outright lies pervaded the whole country. Scholars, intellectuals and the wealthy left the country one by one. Lavish banquets were held in honor of military commanders who came from the frontline. They did not care if these commanders had won or lost the battles, they just wanted to party. Leaders made decisions based on false reports full of flattery hailing them as the *crème de la crème*. Some believed they were protected by divine powers and started to place their faith in superstition. When they finally woke up, it was too late. The people from the lower and middle classes could not stand the Khmer Republicans any longer. They threw their support behind the incorruptible Revolutionary Khmer or the Liberation Khmer (also known as the Khmer Rouge), which claimed loyalty to Samdech Norodom Sihanouk.

On 27 January 1973 in Paris, the Americans signed an agreement with the North Vietnamese to end their bombing of Vietnam. Following this event, the Americans lost interest in their ally, the Khmer Republicans, from mid-June 1973 onwards. Instead, they became preoccupied with how best to withdraw from the Vietnam War.

Hell Unleashed

The day that we eagerly awaited finally came.

It was 17 April 1975 when the Khmer Rouge forces arrived in Phnom Penh. General Mey Sichan, Chief of Staff of the Khmer Republican forces, announced over the national radio that they were in talks with the Khmer Rouge and urged all Republican soldiers to put down their weapons. In the broadcast, an angry voice could be heard in the background refuting him, saying, "We obtained complete victory through our weapons..." (meaning: our victory was obtained by force, not by negotiation).

Cambodians were happy and proud of the victory and hoped that, henceforth, the country would be peaceful, clean of corruption and free.

At that time, my family and I were staying near a market named Psar Nimet Kun Damrei on National Road Number 5, about six kilometers from Poipet province. We lived in a village in the northwest of the country, far from the capital. We had no information about what was happening in Phnom Penh as the national radio encountered some technical problems and soon shut down. After a while, it was restored and started broadcasting revolutionary music and songs, as well as announcements for missing people. The villagers and the local armed forces waited impatiently for the friendly Khmer Rouge troops' arrival to exert control, but a few days passed by without seeing a single Khmer Rouge soldier. The civil servants returned to their offices hoping to get some news, while rumors started to spread that the wealthy were fleeing to Thailand.

On the morning of the fourth day, the well-organized Khmer Rouge forces came in along the border. They quickly shut down all the border checkpoints and prohibited anyone from entering or leaving. They told all the senior bureaucrats to put on their official regalia to go and receive Samdech Sihanouk in Battambang province. Many obliged and were transported by trucks from Poipet.

One hour later, a *remorque* driver returned and whispered that all those high-ranking officials who got on the trucks were killed at Bat Trang village. We became fearful after hearing about this appalling act by the Khmer Rouge forces, whom before this we had considered our friends. The next day, the Khmer Rouge evicted all of us to the countryside. We were forced to leave the towns for the rural areas, from Ou Chrov (Poipet) near the Thai border to remote villages in the country such as Ta Kong village, Ou Veng village, Sai Samorn village, Chro Neuk village and Anlong Samnor village.

My family and I moved without hesitation in the direction indicated by the Khmer Rouge soldiers. We hoped that we would know a new society, one free from corruption and war, even though the forced evacuation was very harsh.

Along the way, we heard that the Khmer Rouge had killed wealthy businessmen, people who defied their orders and those who deviated from the road. Moreover, they tricked the customs or immigration police officers into stepping forward by telling them that they would be reinstated to their former official positions, while teachers were told to come forward to help with the population census. These officials and teachers disappeared, and were said to have gone for re-education. In actual fact, they were all killed.

Day after day, we became weaker and weaker because we had to walk long distances under the hot April sun from dawn to dusk and were allowed to rest only for meals. Our food supplies were also quickly diminishing even though we tried to conserve as much as we could.

Before leaving Nimet village, I had sought help from a family with a tractor, to let my sickly aged father and my wife, who was looking after our toddlers, ride on it. I would continue the journey on foot with my two other sons. My family and I reunited at Koub Toich village in the afternoon, where we ate some food that we had brought from home. We agreed to assemble again at Ta Kong village and continued our journey in the same manner.

That evening, I arrived in Ta Kong village with my two sons and the other evacuees who had walked. I immediately went searching for the rest of my family but my father, wife and small children were missing. The tractor ferrying them was nowhere to be found.

Together with the other evacuees, my two sons and I stayed in Ta Kong village for three days, waiting anxiously for news from the rest of my family. Due to the large number of displaced people, the Khmer Rouge divided us into small groups to be relocated to different villages. We were assigned with some families we knew to a place called Tumnob Ta Bay, about two kilometers from Ta Kong village. After another day without any news from the rest of my family, I decided to take a risk by going to look for them. I managed to borrow a bicycle and set off at dawn the following day, leaving my eldest and fifth sons, who had walked with me to Ta Kong village, with a family there.

I figured that since the last place we had been together was Koub Toich village, where all seven members of the rest of my family – my father, wife, four small children and a young maid – had set off on the tractor towards the east, I should return to Koub Toich village first, as I was unfamiliar with this region. When I arrived there, I met a family that I had known since we first moved to Nimet. Through them, I found out that the tractor was owned by Towkay (Teochew, meaning "Boss") Soon. He was a Laotian born in Banteay Neang village. They said Towkay Soon had probably driven the tractor to his native village which was in the east, corroborating the other accounts I had been given.

This family gave me a pack of rice and a boiled duck egg with a little salt to sustain me on my journey. I stopped frequently to ask about the tractor's route. Someone told me that, four days before, he had seen a tractor full of passengers and goods going towards the east. The tractor had traveled along the forest fringe in the north. When he said "north," though, he pointed to the east. I continued my journey eastward until I passed the villages of Kut Sot Samroang, Sai Samorn and Cham Naum, until Rohat Teuk village, where I lost the trail of the tractor. In this village, most of the residents were Laotians. I asked for Towkay Soon, but none of the villagers professed to know him. I sensed that all of them were hiding the information from me, so I had to be more tactful. Hence, I said that Towkay Soon had sent me here to deliver a message to his wife. Immediately, a Laotian guided me to the house where she stayed, merely twenty meters from where we were. Clearly, these people knew how to protect the members of their own community.

When I saw my father, wife and four children again, the repressed feelings inside each of our hearts erupted like a volcano. We were too overwhelmed and choked with emotion to speak. Only tears gushed out from our eyes, wetting our cheeks. In the evening, we sat down to deliberate our options for dealing with the troubling situation, with Towkay Soon leading the discussion. At the end of this confidential meeting, we decided to return to Ta Kong village that very night, with the help of a guide named Loeur who would help us to avoid the Khmer Rouge patrol.

Towkay Soon was a kind and far-sighted man. He advised me to take my family to Thailand the following night with his family, but I was hesitant.

Firstly, I did not think the Khmer Rouge would keep killing people, as they needed manpower to restore the country.

Secondly, I thought that the Khmer Rouge leaders could not be cruel barbarians. They were scholars who had studied in western countries and some were my teachers whom I knew to be kind, honest and gentle. Moreover, Samdech Norodom Sihanouk was their leader, and he was clever and would not allow killing of his people. I also imagined that the people who were killed were probably former soldiers or corrupt officials whom the Khmer Rouge hated. These were my thoughts then, based on incorrect assumptions made from the start of the Khmer Rouge victory.

Thirdly, even though Towkay Soon and his wife appeared to be well-meaning and trustworthy, I did not know them well and was not ready to depend on a new acquaintance to decide my future and that of my family.

Fourthly, I did not have the heart to abandon my birthplace at the first hint of trouble without a fight. Instead, I wanted to be part of the Great Leap Forward and participate in the rebuilding of my country under the upright and honest guidance of the Khmer Rouge.

The next day, we heard that Towkay Soon and his family had left Ta Kong village towards the west.

My family and I voluntarily traveled with others to Ou Veng village, about three kilometers from Ta Kong village, into an area called Roniem Daun Sam. The place showed no signs of previously having been inhabited. A total of about ten families arrived at Ou Veng at around ten in the morning that day. We elected the oldest among us as our village chief. The heads of all the families met together to study the geography of this place in order to establish a new village. Each family chose a plot. There were no remains of an old village, such as wood that could be recycled to build our houses. To the east there was a big hill and a natural river about five meters wide and around fifty meters long. The river was not deep but the water was murky so its bed could not be seen. Around a hundred meters to the west, there was a big valley with many *kok dok penh* – a species of sedge commonly woven into chairs – growing in numerous small ponds. These ponds had muddy water and the strong stench of wild boars, as if the beasts had wallowed in them. As we were famished, we took the water from these ponds to make our food. We built our house on the hill to avoid the floods during the rainy season. The valley was close to a forest and we had a water source not far from Ta Kong village.

We frantically set about building our houses as the rainy season was fast approaching (the rainy season starts in May/June and ends around October). We were at the end of the month of *Jak*, according to the Khmer calendar. The skies had started to gather dark and heavy clouds. Soon, the rains would arrive. The rainy season normally starts on the first day of *Roy* and ends on the fifteenth day of *Kdert*, for a duration of four months. Those families previously living in Ta Kong village went back to dismantle their old houses and recycled the building materials to build new ones here. Those of us who came from afar, like my family, had to go into the forest to gather construction materials. My wife harvested reeds, which she tied together to thatch the roof. My two eldest sons went to fetch and filter water from the many small ponds to supply the whole family. My father was sick and could not do much, but he was nonetheless our most important advisor. I armed myself with a very long sickle and tied an ax to my waist using a *krama* (traditional Cambodian scarf). Thus equipped, I began conquering Roniem Daun Sam forest. Despite being the son of a farmer from Srang mountain (in Kampong Speu), this was the first time I had ever been attired thus. I had left my native village when I was twelve to avoid the fierce fighting against the French forces by the anti-colonial groups of Khmer Issarak and Sarang Vong.

Life in the Wild

At that time, I struggled valiantly to eke out a living for my family and me. I did this not out of fear of the Khmer Rouge, even though our living conditions were very arduous; I willingly complied with their orders because I did not want to create problems for them on their revolutionary path. I trusted them because they were renowned and popular with the honest and educated people in power. Samdech Norodom Sihanouk (a nationalist), Hou Youn, Hu Nim, Khieu Samphan, Chuon Mom and other intellectuals who had studied in France were their leaders.

I was fed up with the royalist Sangkum Reastr Niyum (Popular Socialist Party) regime and the Khmer Republic, both characterized by rampant corruption and nepotism. The arrival of the Khmer Rouge heralded new hope for the country with their promise of a new, honest and corruption-free society. As a youth, I had attended lectures by progressive intellectuals and was impressed by their convincing rhetoric and policies to resist the monarchy and the Americans.

With my own bare hands and help from my wife, children and sickly father, we built a big house high from the ground. We were exceedingly happy and proud because we had built it from scratch by ourselves. Despite a complete lack of the usual construction tools or materials such as nails or wires, we accomplished the task using tree trunks, thatches and vines from the forest.

At the end of the seventh month of the Khmer calendar (approximately between May and June), the rainy season started. We raked the rice field before daybreak and then planted rice seeds to make a one-hectare paddy, even as the rains drenched us thoroughly.

All of us were fully occupied with building our new house, growing rice and finding food every day.

My immediate concerns were starvation and sickness. The food supplies from our old house were being depleted rapidly. We had no more white sugar left. I had eaten most of it while my family hardly tasted any. We had only about ten kilograms of rice left. My eldest son was only ten years old then, but he already knew how to help out with the family's situation. My two oldest boys would dig small holes in the wet soil to obtain water. Besides looking for water, they hunted small animals such as fish, wild frogs, snakes and crickets to supplement our diet. They also gathered many kinds of wild mushrooms. We always asked the village elders if such mushrooms were edible before eating them as we were afraid they might be poisonous. We took bamboo shoots and vines to make soup, which tasted like fish soup. We learned how to survive in the forest by asking the other villagers. We tried very hard to adapt to the rural way of life, but were constantly either looking for food or preparing it.

My father was old and weak with chronic diseases. His edema and hemorrhoids worsened especially when he went without food. Before, he would never eat beef (or fermented fish sauce) to avoid a cow being slaughtered to feed him, but since our arrival here, he had started asking for beef. I still had some medicines left so I treated him with vitamins and diuretics.

I too suffered from a malady. I would get very bad gastric pains especially when I was hungry. I had treated myself with Bismuth salts previously but now my supply had ran out. Whenever I experienced these agonizing attacks, I wished to die rather than to live with the unbearable pain. Only the desire to ensure my family's survival kept me going.

Every morning after getting up from bed, I walked deep into the big forest far from our house to defecate. I also took the opportunity to search for anything edible, such as mushrooms or small animals.

On the morning of 8 July 1975, I witnessed a most horrific scene that has haunted me ever since. Goosebumps still appear whenever I have flashbacks of that most savage incident. I was looking for a kind of mushrooms that my sons used to take back when I heard gunshots from the north, about two hundred meters away from me. I glanced in the direction of the gunshots and was stupefied by the violent and cruel scene I witnessed.

On the vast plain with scattered large trees that we had grown fond of, soldiers dressed in all black were firing at people clothed in different colors. The victims – men and women, young and old – fell successively like dominoes onto the ground from the bullets sweeping at them. Little boys were stabbed with bayonets or beaten with rifle butts. Some were viciously smashed against the tree trunks. This horrendous brutality of the Khmer Rouge troops against approximately two hundred innocent people who had tried to flee from their forced evacuation lasted about ten minutes. I learned the number of victims from those villagers mobilized to bury the corpses. From that day onwards, I increasingly understood the truly vile and vicious nature of the Khmer Rouge that considered evacuees like me and my family the "17 April people," or prisoners of war. They could kill us anytime they liked with impunity, without any justification, due process or restraint.

One night, my gastritis flared up very badly. My wife tried to help by pressing down on my abdomen to reduce the pain, but this did not alleviate my condition. My last and only resort was to appeal to supreme spiritual help from my late master named Morm, the abbot of Tror Piang Andeouk pagoda. I was completely exhausted and quickly fell asleep.

In my dream, I saw a very old man walking towards me. He extended his hand to give me a few pieces of a small tree branch that he wanted me to swallow. I did as he said and, suddenly, I woke up feeling better. My gastric pain was gone. I regretted not asking the old man in my dream the name of the tree from which those small pieces came, so that I could have them available before my next attack. I returned to sleep and saw the same old man again. I ran to him and asked for the name of the tree. He told me to follow him to where he would show me the tree. When we reached our destination, he continued on his way and disappeared. The tree that he showed me was approximately two arm-spans in circumference and had died a long time ago. It was completely black and had collapsed into a pool of water, where it was submerged. In the dream, I walked along its trunk until I came to the end of a small branch on the water surface. This was the branch that had cured me. I realized that this was a *danghet* (a species of senna) tree. I wondered why the old man had led me to such a huge tree. If it was indeed a *danghet* tree, why was it was so big? Was the old man trying to explain to me that it was the large *danghet* tree? In northwestern Cambodia, there are two species of this tree: large and small. Near my village, there was only one such tree that belonged to the big species. As for the small species, it is called *sondeak khmaoich*.

When I woke up, I asked my eldest son Naga to cut some branches of the large *danghet* tree at the mouth of the river to the southeast of our house. After a while, he returned with a branch as instructed. I did not know how to use this branch as medicine, so I just chopped it into round thin slices and boiled them in water to make a decoction. Then I drained the liquid and sipped it slowly until I finished it. A few hours later, I again started to feel sick in the stomach, but the pain felt different this time. I had diarrhea. I ran into the forest to defecate. I continued to take this herbal remedy like tea but my diarrhea did not abate until nightfall. Completely exhausted from the diarrhea, I slumped in bed, drowsy until the next morning.

Another Long March

On the morning of 12 July 1975, I was still suffering from diarrhea and had to run to the forest repeatedly. I squatted in the bushes to defecate, which was how we all relieved ourselves in the village. Suddenly, a troop of armed Khmer Rouge soldiers walked into the village and started shooting into the air, bellowing, "Get out of your house quickly! The Siam (Thai) army has entered already. Hurry up!"

I hurriedly ran from the forest to my house and saw a group of three Khmer Rouge soldiers standing in front of it with guns lifted straight at my wife, shouting, "Don't take anything before leaving the house, just yourselves. Move it!"

My wife stood rigidly at the mouth of the staircase. Her hand held the medical kit that contained the medicines and some tools that I needed to make house calls.

Bang!

Without any warning, one of the Khmer Rouge soldiers had fired a shot, narrowly missing my wife. I yelled at her to drop flat onto the ground immediately and not to take any belongings.

As for the group of Khmer Rouge soldiers, they hollered at my wife, "You want to die, eh?"

My wife quickly dropped to the ground, her arms gathering whatever was within reach. Then she took our children by their hands and led them out. I hastily went to support my feeble father, slinging across my shoulders whatever belongings I could take.

All of us were forced to abandon our village that day, just as our rice fields were starting to turn a lush green.

Hian (Teochew, meaning "elder brother") Srun was my neighbor. His family was waiting at the road junction, hoping to hitch a ride on a cart. He had been ill for the past two days with a serious bout of hemorrhoids and had become anemic. I had a box with four ampoules of 0.04 Vitamin D. I injected him with two ampoules and he felt slightly better. His diarrhea abated but he was still losing blood. He found an ox cart willing to take him and all his small children with some of his belongings. We had similar responsibilities, as he, like me, had many children. I asked him to let my sick father ride on the cart with him. I was relieved that my father did not have to walk. I carried our belongings and held the hands of my young children while my wife managed the three youngest toddlers and a bag of things. We left Ta Kong village, passed Tumnob Ta Bay and headed directly for Koub Toich village.

We started to feel hungry because it was lunch time already. Our group of villagers had gone far ahead of us. They left my father on the roadside to wait for us as we had arrived late. Someone whispered to me not to walk too slowly or the Khmer Rouge could kill us. My family and I tried our best to continue our journey as quickly as we could. The sky turned dark and soon rain started pounding on us. From small raindrops at first, it soon became a heavy storm. Initially, the light rain provided relief from the heat and we felt cool and comfortable. We regained some energy, but after a longer time, its relentless hammering made us freezing cold and barely able to lift our feet. My father's and small children's faces turned ashen and their teeth began to chatter.

I carried my father piggyback while taking care of our belongings as well. I would place my father on my back and carry him some distance, the put him down and turn back to collect our things, which I would carry to where he was before repeating this sequence. I managed in this way throughout our journey. To make matter worse, the road was bumpy and slippery. With my father on my back, I had fallen many times into the rice fields. It was exceedingly strenuous and I ran out of breath. Nonetheless, I pushed on valiantly because I had to fulfill my obligation as a son, a husband and a father, so giving up was out of question. This resolve spurred me on.

Observing my fatigue from this tedious labor, my father stopped me from carrying him again. He told me to leave him in the shack near the road junction. He reasoned that even if I could take him along, he would still die eventually, so it was better to let him die alone inside that shack. The lives of his small grandchildren should have priority over his life. I begged him not to give up hope but he was adamant. Then some Khmer Rouge soldiers came and ordered me to move along. I pleaded with them for some time to convince my father to come with me.

My father reproached me for not listening to him. A few days before this second evacuation, he had told me to take him and my family to Thailand as soon as possible. As he could not walk far, he suggested that I borrow a villager's water buffalo. By tying him to the back of the water buffalo, he was sure that I would be able to transport him and my family safely to Thailand. Moreover, he said that, if the Khmer Rouge soldiers chased us, I should release the water buffalo with him on its back and flee for our own lives without looking back. Had I listened to him then, we would not have been in this predicament today. He also scolded me for my indecisiveness.

When he had stopped his scolding, I urged him to continue the journey on my back. The Khmer Rouge soldiers were watching us because we were far behind the rest of the group. I appealed to my father many times, but he was cantankerous. Finally, I decided that with him unable to go on any farther, I could not abandon him even though we would surely be killed by the Khmer Rouge soldiers. I told him, "We will die here together because as your son, I cannot let them shoot my old father in the middle of the road like this." Immediately, my father changed his mind.

It rained cats and dogs. All of our teeth started chattering. My father was on my back. My wife had wrapped our baby with a *krama* around her bosom but he was so cold that his lips had turned purple. We had very little hope of enduring this situation for much longer because it rained incessantly. Fatigued and breathless, we could barely lift our feet and we were thirsty and hungry too. We had not eaten since the prior evening.

Evening arrived and it turned really dark. Our numbed legs strained to move forward mechanically. Shortly after, we reached the Koub Toich village temple where we seemed to regain some strength. My wife asked me for the clay jar of salt inside the basket of things that I had taken from the house. This jolted me, as I had thrown away all our things without knowing what they contained because they were too heavy. My father and I had fallen over on our stomachs from a dike into a paddy field full of muddy water. My wife whispered that she had hidden all our gold and diamonds under the salt in that jar. All our valuables were now gone forever! She started to weep, as all these possessions had been accumulated from our labors of blood, toil, tears and sweat over many years.

People massed on the field of the pagoda. Our legs were full of sticky mud. Everyone rushed to take the dry bamboo mats from inside the pagoda to rest on. By now, the rain had finally stopped. Only small droplets fell on us here, but there was hardly any available space. We were packed like sardines.

My wife sought a place where she could nurse the baby. I wanted a dry patch to put my father down from my back. Walking a little farther, we saw a small elevated hut camouflaged by thatch. We walked towards it. It was surrounded by homeless, exhausted people like us because its sturdy columns supported them. My wife and I stopped enduring. She leaned on a pillar of the hut for support to breastfeed our baby. I squatted to let my father down on the mud. I dragged some thatch to spread on top of the mud so that we could rest. We were truly depleted as we had not eaten since the evening before and now it was too late to go searching for food. I called my eldest sons to ask for food from the other people but to remember the way back so that they would not get lost. They left as instructed. I was close to tears watching their small bodies depart and also from seeing my father asleep on the thatch on the mud.

I could not bear this suffering anymore. My chest was constricted to the point of suffocation. To release the pressure, I yelled out, "Oh! Do divine beings have eyes or not? They see me so miserable yet they do not help me!"

I had just finished shouting when I heard someone in the hut asking, "Whose voice was it? It sounded like the doctor."

I responded at once, "Doctor says not doctor." (In the local dialect, this means: "Of course, it's the doctor.")

Just then, the door of the hut swung open. A man about my age approached me. Then he returned to the hut and said, "Yes, it's really the doctor."

Shortly after, he gave me a bowl filled to the brim with rice, whispering, "Doctor, I came to work as the Organization's driver. They gave me a house here for some time already. I only have one bowl of sticky rice left. I hope it is enough for Doctor to satisfy your hunger." I thanked him profusely for he had come to my rescue at a time of dire need.

(The Organization here refers to the Khmer Rouge. In Khmer, it is called "Ongkar" but usually anglicized as "Angkar.")

I gave one part of the rice to my father. He held up both his hands to receive it, trembling from the cold but also from overwhelming joy. My children returned empty-handed to inform me, "Pa! I asked for food from the others but failed to receive any." I divided the rice into equal parts for my wife, children and myself. It then struck me that I should give that man all five goslings that I had slung across my shoulder from my house at Ou Veng to thank him, since I could not bear their weight any longer.

I discussed this idea with my wife who let me decide. I took all five goslings to that man. I informed him that I had come to give him all these goslings because I could not continue my journey with so many loads on me, including my father, my small children and many things. He took them from my hands without a word.

Around midnight, he came with a big pot of porridge for me. Then he left and returned with another pot of salted goose meat and a pair of trousers, whispering politely, "Doctor, I have nothing to give you except to make salted goose meat to sustain you on your journey." With that, he went back into the hut most quietly.

I will always remember the kindness and good heart of that man.

I scooped a bowl of porridge for my father and gave an equal portion to Hian Srun. My whole family and I agreed to let the rest of Hian Srun's family and two other elderly persons finish the remaining porridge.

All the children from both our families concurred that the food we had received was heavenly because it provided sustenance for our lives, especially for the two sick persons – my father and Hian Srun.

Regretfully, I never found out the identity of my benefactor. During the revolution, we were not free to establish friendship as the Organization had cut off all relationships between people. That kind man took a huge risk by giving us food. He had to do it furtively because the consequences would have been grave if he were caught.

Around two hours after midnight, the loudspeakers started blaring. We got up and moved to the railway station as instructed. On the railway tracks were carriages left open for us to board. Shortly after, the thunderous sounds of the train moving forward echoed forth. Another two hours later, the train came to a quiet stop. They ordered us to descend. We slid down from the train onto the railway track in the impenetrable darkness. We huddled together tightly, groping and blindly feeling our way until we came to the road beneath. Immediately, the stench of human excrement engulfed us. We endured here, waiting for dawn. My father slept leaning on our sack of clothes and things. My children snuggled silently together on our pile of things. When dawn broke, I woke my family up just when my father cleared his throat. We followed the group of people in front of us. I supported my father and slung things across my shoulders. When necessary, I carried him on my back. My wife carried the youngest children and balanced on her head our sack of clothes. The older children carried pails and pots. We were afraid to step on the feces so we walked on the railway track instead. Even so, it was also full of shit.

About two hundred meters away, we came to National Road Number 5. There were many vehicles, *remorques* and tractors waiting here to transport us *en masse* to different places as allocated by the Organization.

My family stopped to rest at the entrance of the former agricultural bureau of this village named Chrouy Sdau because my father was completely drained and could not continue. A group of soldiers came to pressurize us to leave, but upon seeing my father's strained condition, they left to urge the others instead. People left one by one until the place was almost empty. I heard that some went to Nikom village, some to Kouk Khmum village, while others to Kean Ker Sar village. Only my family and I were stranded. We had to wait for my father to regain some energy to continue our journey. I did not know this place at all but I started wondering, even when my father had regained his strength, where and how we would go now that all the vehicles transporting the people were gone?

We obtained water to cook rice for lunch and decided to wait a while before we continued on our way. After my wife and children had finished cooking the rice and a portion of the salted goose meat, I scooped a plate of rice with a little grilled goose meat for my father. My family and I shared one big plate together. The food was delicious to us because we were ravenous.

By late afternoon, my father appeared a bit stronger but I wavered between moving on and staying here for a night. I was at wits' end when I saw my close friend from Nimet named Yi approaching me. He told me that he had asked the chief of Toul Kork village to let us stay there, together with my younger cousin's family. We quickly set off for Toul Kork village.

Toul Kork village was not far from Chrouy Sdau village. We moved as quickly as we could, according to my father's ability. I supported him and carried our belongings too. Each of us had had to shoulder some responsibility since we had left on this journey. We walked along the bank of a canal alongside the garden belonging to the former chief of the Cambodian Development Center for about one kilometer. Then we turned right into a road for another kilometer to reach Toul Kork village.

The village was located on a small hill of approximately thirty meters squared in area, which had a creek about the width of a road. About ten families had been evicted from Chrouy Sdau village and relocated here. The whole village was arranged around the circumference of the hill. In the center was a shelter that was also used as a cow shed, a kitchen-cum-canteen and a meeting hall.

When we arrived, the villagers let us rest inside this communal shelter. Immediately, some young women lunged forward to search our things. We did not know what they were looking for. One of them lifted our bag of remaining rice and shrieked, "Confiscate!" but the village chief rebuffed her, "Let him keep it, he has many children!"

At that time, I noticed my father gesturing and pointing to himself, but I did not understand what he wanted to say. Later, I found out that my father had hidden all his money under the rice in that bag. There was only a little rice left and a big wad of 500-riel notes underneath it. My father signaled to let me know that if they discovered the money, I should reply that he was the one who had put it there. Luckily, they did not empty the rice from the bag. Instead, they put their creeping hands into our clothes to search for any valuables we may have hidden on us.

If we were caught making any mistake such as hiding personal property, we would be punished. Punishment could range from light penalties such as slapping or beating, to the ultimate, which was death by execution. Thankfully, they did not find anything on us.

I was shocked and shaken by this experience because all these women were victims like us, the "17 April people" that the Organization had liberated from the previous regime. Why did they turn on us so maliciously, like we were their enemies or war prisoners sent by the Organization? It had been only three months, yet the Khmer Rouge's bloodthirsty ideology had seeped into the blood vessels of all of them.

I was dumbfounded by the brutality of the Khmer Rouge youth. I dared not look any one of them directly in the eye because I was scared of the power they wielded, which they abused with impunity due to their ignorance and crudeness. The Khmer Rouge could be compared to evil spirits that possessed Khmer children to spill the blood of all Khmers until it ran completely dry. They took in only uneducated, unthinking youngsters who could easily be manipulated to become the group's shadowy executioners. These youngsters lorded over the indigenous people who had stayed in the same villages for generations. They treated the populace as enemies of the revolution, totally disregarding kinship, even their own parents or blood relatives. The Khmer Rouge recognized only the community of laborers and farmers. The Organization's theories and practices should simply be recognized as sheer madness because ordinary people were incapable of such evil and abhorrent behaviors.

They killed people because they were scared that the people would kill them. After killing people for a long time, they were still dissatisfied and started killing each other. Surely such sick behaviors were the acts of crazy psychopaths? There is an old Khmer saying that:

Those who kill other people sometimes
get blood into their eyes.
Such people see others only as prey for them to kill.

It means that a murderer, having killed once, develops a propensity to kill again, like an addiction.

Ash to Ash

We stayed for a short time under the roof of that communal shelter. Two days later we moved our things into a hut near a rice field to the south of the hill.

We built this hut carelessly and hastily based on whatever materials we could find just to shelter us from the weather. My wife went in search of thatch to make the roof while my children and I went to look for wooden planks.

We tried our best to get along with the others who were laborers and farmers but they were not friendly with us. They treated us with contempt because we were city dwellers the Organization despised.

We labored hard and dared not neglect our duties. We learned to plant rice, build dams, dig trenches, carry sacks of rice on our shoulders, sieve rice and transplant rice seedlings like the others. All these manual labors that we had never done previously completely exhausted us. After a rainy and windy day working in the paddy, where we were soaked in water and mud, we were so exhausted we could hardly walk. Our hands and legs ached terribly. Later, the village chief assigned me to work in the kitchen, so I had to get up at three in the morning. I had to start the fire to make the watery gruel that we ate for breakfast daily, by boiling five small cans of rice inside a pot, about two feet in diameter, which Cambodians traditionally used to caramelize palm juice to make sugar. At five in the morning, people would come for their breakfast before leaving for work and return in the evening for another meal.

At that time, the Organization was not very strict so we could still use any spare time to look for other food to fill our stomachs. After making the porridge, I cleaned the kitchen, split logs and transported water in pails suspended from both ends of a pole that I carried across my shoulder.

We were required to eat together in the canteen. We stopped having any private possessions, except our old clothes and a spoon each. We stomped on our new clothes until they became dull in color to prevent them from looking beautiful. We hid any valuables we had from the sight of the Organization or soldiers who would otherwise confiscate them and accuse us of all manner of crime. We had to obey them. They could accuse us of being anti-revolutionary and send us for re-education. Our situation was hopeless and our future bleak.

My father's health improved slightly and he tried to find some light labor in the village that he could do. My two eldest sons joined the youth mobile units. My third child, a girl, looked after the younger children inside the communal circle.

The medicines for my father were running out. Previously, I injected him once every two days, then once every three days and finally, once every five days. By the end of August, there was no more. I informed him of this tragic fact. He became despondent and withdrawn as he lost hope of living much longer. Every time I returned from work, he would chat with me and remind me not to neglect myself. He told me to actualize myself as a brave man and, should an opportunity arise, to flee from this regime. He requested that upon his death, if there were enough firewood, his corpse should be cremated completely so that there would be nothing left behind, because the communists did not allow people to pay respect to their ancestors. If there were no firewood for a cremation, he wanted his body to be buried deeply, about one and a half to two meters deep into the soil to avoid others digging at his grave.

From then onwards, my father started to lose weight. He became very gaunt but his legs were swollen, making them look very fat. I could not help my father anymore under such circumstances.

A few days later, he could no longer walk and stayed on the bamboo mat the whole day. At night, I slept with him and we chanted the Buddhist sutras softly (the Organization had outlawed religion). I recounted the Buddha's life story and when I made a mistake, he corrected me. During the day, I sneaked back to check on him whenever I could.

On the night of 3 September 1975, one of his legs became infected with oozing pus, leaving only scorched black skin on his lower calf. The following night, the gangrene afflicted the other leg too.

At four in the morning of 5 September 1975, my father left us forever.

He departed during a monsoon with very heavy rains. Many places were flooded and the torrential deluge obscured the daylight, engulfing us in a grim, gloomy atmosphere.

I decided to cremate his body on a small hillock. My neighbors came to pay their last respects. They also helped to make a coffin and to prepare his body for the final rites.

Around eight in the morning, we carried the coffin with my late father inside, using a pole supported on the shoulders of two men. We took turns to transport the coffin as we searched for a suitable dry spot but could not find any. At last, Brother Soon decided that the intersection of the two big dikes would do, even though it was also submerged in water. We heaped mud to raise the land so that the coffin could be placed on top. Then we piled firewood on the coffin before igniting it. The fire burned until only ashes and charcoal remained. I did not have the heart to completely heed my father's words to cremate his body until there was nothing left. To the contrary, I was determined to keep some of his remains for veneration in the future (this is a common Asian practice of ancestral worship). Later I asked my wife to help me separate the ashes into three small sachets. One sachet was for me and the other two for each of my two eldest sons.

In the end, only the sachet with me remained. The other two sachets were lost when the Thai troops forced my family down the Preah Vihear Mountain.

Life inside the Cooperative

From November 1975 onwards, the Organization mobilized approximately one hundred families to form a cooperative called "Snuol Kaong Cooperative," straddling around two kilometers on both sides of the garden belonging to the former chief of the Cambodian Development Center.

The cooperative comprised of four villages: Toul Kork, Snoul Kaong, Ou Pror Keab and Kouk Pradak. All four villages shared three communal kitchens ("Food Circles"), which were also called "worksites." The chief was a man called Chief Dum. The assistant chief was called Grandfather Chan. We did not call him chief because he was very old, and so we addressed him as "Grandfather" or "Uncle" instead. There was a member named Cheay and four other couples who were their assistants.

Inside the cooperative, there was a spy unit that collected information on us. The chief was named Yay. He had many spies under his command.

All these leaders had distinguished themselves as crusaders of the revolution. They had the power to propose the appointment of new people to become chiefs of various units or groups.

The executive committee at Snuol Kaong Cooperative was predominantly local with a small minority from Thailand or Laos who came from Kdol Tahen village. Around the middle of 1978, the Khmer Rouge from the southwest (headed by Ta Mok) took all of them away for re-education.

Inside the cooperative, my family members were assigned work individually. I worked at the communal hospital and the plantation. My wife was involved in paddy farming. My two eldest sons and my first daughter were in the youth mobile units. My fourth and fifth sons were in the mobile unit for children. My sixth son was just a toddler and was taken care of by two grandmothers (we called all the elderly women in the cooperative "grandmothers") in the canteen during the day. In the evenings, my wife would pick him up when she had finished her work.

I was completely nauseated to see my children doing forced labor near the canal every day, especially my eldest daughter. They assigned her to build a very big dam near the cooperative. She was only seven years old then but they made her carry on her head a two-handled basket full of soil to fill the back of a dam, which was about three meters high. She walked back and forth to collect the soil. My daughter was the only one who wore red trousers because she did not have black pants like the other children. I could clearly see my daughter working even from a distance because of her red slacks. My heart ached and tears flowed in commiseration of my children's unfortunate destiny.

The Revolutionary Organization created many new words. They invented terms for propaganda, for receiving orders, for establishing contact, for seeking pardon, for interrogation or denunciation, and for making announcements. It seemed to be a technique of the revolution.

All of us were isolated from each other. Each division had a total of three persons: a chief, an assistant and a member. Many divisions constituted a group. There was no limit on the number of people in a group, which could range from a few to many. Forced labor was carried out through units. For example, we had the plowing unit, the harvest unit, the unit to transplant seedlings, the mining unit, the unit to look for soil, the unit to raise the canal and the mobile unit. Doctors who prepared herbs and treated diseases were called "community teachers." The fishing unit was called "group harvesters."

Each unit was further divided into sections according to their function or rank and they were separated from each other. Within each section, there was a leader in direct control.

Each group had accountability to an individual designated as the "Chief appointed by the Organization." The phrase "to receive personal responsibility" meant that if there was a problem, the person concerned had to shoulder the consequences, which could include execution because the Khmer Rouge reportedly did not have prisons or detention centers in the villages. In any case, none of us could verify this claim. If the leaders or spies caught anyone contravening the Organization's laws, they would take this person to the Chief appointed by the Organization. Even if the accused was innocent, he or she would disappear forever.

Moreover, families of those accused by the Khmer Rouge of a crime could not protest or appeal either. We stopped using the word "enemy" because anyone with a relationship with an enemy was in serious breach of the Organization's laws and would die together with them. If a family member was taken away, the rest of that family would fear for their own lives because they could be implicated next. Hence, each of us carefully kept our distance from other people, even from those we had once been close to, as a precaution. We spoke very little.

The only time that we had to speak without fail was during meetings. Division meetings comprising the three persons were to be held every evening after dinner. Section or unit meetings were called by their respective leaders. We reported to these meetings individually and glumly. People spoke about their own shortcomings such as being lazy, careless or negligent, with such failings contributing to weakening the position of the revolutionary forces against the American Empire and its allies. At the end of the meetings, they asked the leaders for help to correct their flaws so as to become good revolutionaries with the statement, "Just as one cannot see the mud on one's back, if Chief should notice any of my mistakes, please help me to rectify and improve."

At division meetings, each person had to say something individually. The meeting was closed only after all three persons had spoken, and it was only then that we could go home.

Every night, we worried for our lives because that was when the spies came out. Those who were called away during the night often never returned.

The spy unit was separately accountable to its independent leadership. When night fell, the young spies sneaked between the houses to identify those who had not complied with the Organization's laws; who had perpetrated misconduct such as stealing food; or who kept complaining about their suffering inside the cooperative or about their forced labor. These spies would lie down under our houses or lurk behind the corner walls to eavesdrop on us.

The other big meeting was the cooperative meeting. This meeting was held irregularly, according to the Organization's dictates. The purpose was often to propagate or explain the Organization's ideology. Sometimes, it was held to issue new orders or to inform people about national or international developments. At such meetings, the leaders not only exaggerated but told outright lies unabashedly. Perhaps the speakers suspended their better judgment or blindly believed in the stories because they were illiterate.

At one such cooperative meeting, after the rest had spoken, one of them stood up and proclaimed that the American Empire was scared and deeply bewildered because the Americans had no rice to eat now that the Organization refused to sell rice to it. It would face certain death without question because it did not know how to plant rice itself. It only knew how to make airplanes, tanks, guns and cars. Right now, the Organization was selling rice at a high price: one sack of rice in exchange for a tractor. Moving forward, Democratic Kampuchea would not lack tractors. The Organization had therefore stopped supplying oxen to plow the fields because it was satisfied and happy that our lives would be easy and comfortable after such good news.

The whole meeting clapped hands to cheer such uplifting news.

He appeared completely oblivious that something was amiss and elaborated, "The American Empire was defeated by our Organization and what's more, Americans have no rice to eat now."

There were many instances of such rhetoric that should have made us laugh.

On another occasion, a chief spoke on the need to salvage and preserve resources. He related that a leader of the Organization was traveling in a car on a national road one day. This leader saw an iron boundary signpost on the road. He stopped the car and alighted from it to pick up the signpost, despite his busy schedule. After this speech, the cooperative chief allowed us to emulate this leader's example and salvage things.

All these stories permitted no questioning. They were simply to convey the Organization's instructions to the listeners. Would the revolution succeed if the intelligence and ideas of the leadership deteriorated to such low levels?

The big group meetings were comparable to the assemblies of our present-day associations or establishments. They could be to transmit the Organization's ideology, to give directions, to appoint people or to punish people with serious mistakes. Among such mistakes were included immoral behaviors or illicit love affairs that were exposed; betraying the collective by stealing the cooperative's supplies or groceries; intentionally or unintentionally breaking supplies or causing them to spoil; or causing the beasts of burden to die or suffer injury. There were also big group meetings to marry young men and women.

Strike One

Inside this Snuol Kaong Cooperative, I was accused many times.

The first time happened when I asked the Organization for permission to allow the workers in the unit responsible for transplanting the rice seedlings to take the boiled water that I had prepared for them out to drink when they were working in the fields. This way, they would have clean drinking water when they became thirsty while working and thus be protected from various diseases such as dysentery, gastric flu or cholera.

The executive committee accused me of attempting to erase the consciousness of the revolutionary masses by scaring them that they would fall ill if they drank water from the rice fields. They retorted, "Our comrades drank water from the rice fields and defeated the American Empire, so how come our comrades did not die?"

Normally, I would have been hauled in front of a group meeting for the chief to mete out my punishment, but I asked them to give me three months first. If during this time, we did not have any epidemic, I would willingly accept their punishment. Otherwise, if there were to be an epidemic and I was dead already, who would explain to the chief? After listening to my explanation, they acceded to my request.

I also asked for permission to go into the primary forest to collect and stockpile medicinal plants as a precaution. This time, they disagreed but they sent some other people to go in my place. The medicinal plants included: *ongtok* (Long Jack, popularly known as "tongkat ali" or "Malaysian ginseng"), the bark of the *preah pnao* tree (a species of Cambodian almond tree), *bonraw* (a type of palm), medicinal tubers, and the epiphytic mistletoes growing on the pomegranate and carambola (starfruit) trees. All these medicinal plants were difficult to find here so they had to search in the virgin forest at the old creek where the soil was braided red and white.

More than a month went past before there was a case of diarrhea accompanied by severe vomiting in Preah Ponlea village and another village bordering it. In my heart, I was relieved, as this meant that I would escape the death penalty due to the immediate danger posed to the general population.

The following night, I received news that Teacher Art, who stayed nearby to the south of my hut had taken ill with severe diarrhea and vomiting. His wife ran to ask for my help to treat him. This man was appointed by the Organization to educate all the children inside the cooperative.

My wife and I hurried to the sick man's hut. He was convulsing and flailing on the bed. I checked his blood pressure with my instrument and his pulse with my hand. His vital signs were barely detectable. I asked his wife about his symptoms. She replied that he had defecated once and vomited many times. According to my experience, these symptoms constituted a medical emergency but there was no hospital to confirm the diagnosis and render treatment. I quickly took the mistletoes from the pomegranate and carambola trees to wash with rice water inside my medicinal pestle. Then I fed it to Teacher Art. After that, I made more of this herbal remedy to let him sip repeatedly. We soon obtained some good signs: his diarrhea and vomiting stopped. I told his relatives and friends who had gathered in his hut to watch over him.

From my experience, this disease is difficult to treat with oral medication because whatever is ingested is immediately spewed out. Approximately half an hour past midnight, I went to measure Teacher Art's blood pressure again. I was relieved to detect his blood pressure, although the pulse readings on his upper arm and thigh were not encouraging.

That night, I treated many more sick people like Teacher Art. The next day, we continuously treated such patients the whole day and night. My wife and I did not rest at all. We treated this disease with the same remedy: washing the mistletoe from the pomegranate and carambola trees with rice water and feeding it to the infirm. This remedy has unbelievable efficacy. Moreover, if the sick person had a bad stomachache, I would take a minute amount of cooked opium that had been preserved with salt using the end of a bamboo skewer, mix it in water and let the sick person drink it. A friend had given me a small pill of this salted opium.

My wife and I successfully treated more than fifty sick persons in the Snoul Kaong cooperative in two nights and one day. I heard that this disease had killed many people in the other cooperatives, wiping out even entire villages. I supplied this remedy to the other cooperatives' community teachers who came to ask for it.

I still marvel at the remarkable effectiveness of this traditional remedy for treating diarrhea and vomiting. However, I have since then never had another chance to further investigate it due to a lack of supporters or believers. My own observations during the famine under the Khmer Rouge regime indicated that traditional medicines have very strong potency, despite my giving only small doses that would be considered insufficient to treat diseases. One of my friends said that, when our stomachs have hunger cramps, any medicine would have a stronger effect than usual. Another friend said that, after our bodies have not used a medicine for a long time, when we take it again, its effects are stronger. Both these friends knew about the success that my wife and I had in treating diarrhea and nausea with this traditional remedy, which was a source of pride for us.

The cooperative chief became jealous of our achievement. We were war prisoners who did not have the honor to experience any success or pride, because only the Revolutionary Organization could receive permanent and resounding success.

I assumed that even if the executive committee did not congratulate me on my accomplishment, they had surely noted it down in their hearts. Nonetheless, I downplayed my success because it could be dangerous for me. Hence, whenever I spoke about this episode, I always paid tribute to the brilliant Organization that had supplied me with this marvelous remedy. My flattery calmed their hearts somewhat and they became friendlier with me than before.

Strike Two

The second time the Organization accused me was because I was too friendly and trusting, especially with one old man named Sut, who was my neighbor and a Kampuchea Krom native.

I had carelessly whispered to Grandfather Sut, "Just be patient and endure. When the tide turns, we will not leave any leftovers, not even a tiny piece, because when the water rises, fish eat ants, but when the water recedes, ants eat fish. This is the natural order."

Not many days later, the cooperative chief dispatched the group chief to call me for a meeting. When I reached the meeting place in the center of a rice field at dusk, it was dark and deadly silent. I could not clearly perceive the attendees at that meeting. I heard the cooperative chief's voice call out that I had committed an infraction the day before.

I started to recite according to the formalities of a group meeting, "I pay my respect to the cooperative chief, the group chief, the unit chiefs and all the leaders of the Organization. All my improper actions that cause them displeasure are unintentional because I am ignorant due to a lack of education in the ways of the revolution and I have not thoroughly eradicated all my old ways. Even so, I try very hard to respect and abide by the laws and orders of the Organization. I do my best to fulfill the quota of three tons of rice from one hectare of paddy, according to the directions from the Organization. I make many mistakes every day but I cannot see them myself because they are like mud on my back. Therefore I ask all the chiefs for help to please correct me in order to advance forward together."

When I had finished speaking, the assistant chief put to me, "What of the story about fish eating ants when the water is high, and ants eating fish when the water is low?"

I paid my respect to the chiefs again before expressing that I had indeed uttered these words to Uncle Sut (we called old people around the age of our fathers "Uncle" or "Father") because he often complained about the forced labor that the Organization imposed on him; that at his old age, the Organization was still enslaving him. I always counseled him that he had previously been a rich man who led an easy life. Now that the Organization had raised the status of the laborers and farmers, Uncle Sut should not be disgruntled because according to the saying: "When the water is high, the fish eat the ants but when the water is low, the ants eat the fish." He was angry with me for saying this and said that I was an insolent junior who dared to reprimand him. The reason I dared to do so was because the Organization had always taught us to help to improve each other in order to serve the Revolutionary Organization for the greater good together. This was it. If I had made a mistake, I asked all the chiefs to please help correct me and from this point onwards, I would never dare to correct Uncle Sut again.

The chief replied, "Comrade Eng (my name at that time), you did not make any mistake because we help to correct each other in order to improve and advance forward together."

The cooperative chief ended the meeting.

I returned to my hut. My wife, two neighboring old women and a few other elderly were waiting anxiously for me. They stared at me with horror on their faces and asked, "Teacher, how did it go? We are all very scared.

Did the Organization impose anything on Teacher or not?"

I simply answered, "The Organization did not punish me."

They were clearly relieved to hear this and happily returned to their huts.

Close Shaves

1977 had ended and we were into a new year.

My patience had been exhausted. I could not endure it anymore. I was besieged with fear and worry, searching for a way to free myself and the people from the evil Khmer Rouge regime. My father's advice before his death to flee from this regime and to let my children live in a free country echoed repeatedly in my ears.

My youngest daughter was only a few months old. As a father, I had to make the painful decision to forsake my children to escape alone. My plan to steal firearms from the Khmer Rouge before fleeing had to be abandoned when my friends postponed its implementation. I started to fret that it had been leaked.

All these questions made me extremely jittery and anxious.

I was assigned by the Organization to take care of the plantation. I planted vegetables and tobacco on the bank of the canal near the dam. Previously, there had been two temples located side by side here, but these were now completely devastated. The Organization ordered me to destroy one of these temples to obtain clay for making a stove. (Another team was assigned to destroy the other temple.) I was completely aghast that the chief was punishing me to annihilate this ancient holy temple site. I was petrified to violate our ancestors' sacred temples. Until today, I regret deeply that one of these temples was destroyed by my own hands.

Destroying the temple was akin to cutting my own body. It pained me badly, but how could I defy the Organization's orders?

I went alone to the temple that I was tasked to destroy. Before starting work, I took three small twigs to replace incense sticks and, after lighting them, I stuck them into the ground at the temple's doorway and silently paid my highest respect and homage to the spirits. I informed them that I had no choice but to destroy this sacred place with immeasurable historical value, because if I defied the order, the evil Khmer Rouge would surely kill me. I asked for their divine forgiveness and sought their compassionate understanding that I was a war prisoner with no rights. If they were angry, they should direct their wrath at the Khmer Rouge for ordering the destruction of all places of worship. I did this secretly every morning.

After my morning ritual one day, I heard the sound of someone clearing his throat behind me. I quickly turned around and caught sight of the executive committee member named Cheay, but he walked away briskly.

I was extremely scared. I thought my life would soon be over, but there was no reaction at all from him. He was a person of good character: pleasant, modest, gentle and quiet. He took pity on us very much. His wife was also like him. They did not discriminate between the leadership and the rest of us, but treated everyone equally.

I dug at the remains of the temple until they completely disappeared into the ground, covered by dry yellow soil. Under the yellow soil was a kind of insoluble fine white powder. I continued digging until a depth of approximately three meters. I lifted my hands to pay my respect and prayed to the spirits of the ancestors who had built this five-by-five meters temple, which clearly had a magnificent architecture. It was unclear how tall the temple had been, as the roof had collapsed and all that was left was a door made from a hard, solid blue stone. Large surfaces on the door had inscriptions in ancient Khmer script. I buried this door in a hole and dropped other parts of the temple into the nearby canal, hoping that future archeologists would find them one day.

While destroying this temple, I chanced upon a statue of Buddha protected by the mythical dragon-like creatures Khmers called *naga*. It was golden color and was the size of my palm. The heads of two creatures above the Buddha and part of the throne below had decayed. It looked like a very old statue. I was shoveling and about to throw away some debris when I saw a sinking round brick. I thought it strange and reflexively tried to grab it for a closer look. My sudden gesture startled someone nearby named Ran who shouted, "Comrade, found something?"

I replied truthfully that I had found a round brick. While I was bending down to retrieve it, Ran had dashed over to my side and he arrived right on time. We examined that strange piece of round brick together. When I knocked it with a piece of stone near the canal, the metallic yellow color of gold appeared. I was overjoyed to find this golden Buddha statue of an ancient temple, but Ran, who held a revolutionary position, muttered frostily,

"Comrade, are you going to betray the Organization?" He had seen me put the statue into the pocket of my trousers.

I responded that he should not accuse me like that because I was going to hand it over to the Organization when I returned home that evening.

When I arrived home, I took out the statue to show my wife under the fish oil lamp. Both of us greatly admired it but feared for the ancient temple at the same time. I needed to make haste and surrender the statue to the Organization to avoid the sneaky suspicion that Ran had about me.

I caressed and examined the statue with utmost respect and love. Then I took a basin of water and put it on the bed. I prayed, "If this Buddha statue truly has immense power, all the gods please show me now." After that, I put the Buddha statue into the basin of water and went to wake my fifth son up. I sprinkled some water from that basin into his eyes and prayed, "Please heal my child's night blindness." Then I told my son to go outside to urinate by walking across a small bridge over the canal in front of our hut. He set off at once, walking quickly without his habitual hesitation. Before this, I always had to lead him by his hand because he could not see the road or bridge clearly in the dark. On this night, his night blindness was cured.

This was indeed a most miraculous and powerful statue. I took it to the cooperative chief with great sadness and reluctance in my heart. After all these years, I still miss it immensely. When I revisited Snuol Kaong in 2000, the statue's whereabouts could not be ascertained. The ruins of the two isolated temples lay covered by sedges in the middle of some paddy fields.

After tearing down the temple walls, I used the soil I was able to salvage from them to expand the plantation. The powdery soil from the bricks was infertile and had no nutrients. I enlarged the plantation to an area of nearly one *ray* (approximately forty meters squared). I planted vegetables such as cabbage, eggplants, pumpkins and cucumbers, and in the center of the plantation, I planted tobacco. The vegetables did not provide good yields because they were often ruined or eaten by insects or small animals such as rats until there was none left. The pumpkins provided some harvests, but still insufficient to provide energy. We did not have fertilizers or pesticides, so none of the crops grew well. Only the tobacco provided an average supply. I collected the chicken manure from the central coop and people's urine from the hospital to fertilize the tobacco plants.

The tobacco plants grew fabulously with big leaves due to all the nutrients. The enemies of the tobacco plants were the worms that grew inside them, causing them to swell. I had to incise them to extract such worms or else the plants would die or be stunted. The tobacco that I cultivated had a strong, pleasant taste, so some people called me "Grandfather Strong Tobacco."

In a year, the total output of what I strove so hard to grow still could not match the small quantities that the Organization provided for my food. I thought to myself, "I tried so hard to cultivate the crops from dawn to dusk for one full year without any rest days, but only produced such a tiny harvest, totally incommensurable with the energy that I had expended using planting techniques without fertilizers and pesticides." I understood clearly that the general economy of the Khmer Rouge, based on a revolving labor force, was without a doubt doomed to fail.

The Khmer Rouge thought that, previously, the farmers had sustained the city dwellers. The farmers worked very hard but received only a pittance for their labors. The Khmer Rouge supported the farmers, whom they claimed were being oppressed.

As for the city dwellers, they worked very little but received many benefits as the middle men. These people were swindlers who cheated the farmers. They were liars and cheats just waiting to eat without knowing how to farm or to produce anything at all. The Khmer Rouge considered urbanites as the oppressors.

According to their self-proclaimed illuminating and immense ideology, the Revolutionary Organization's Great Leap Forward would reverse this social injustice by mobilizing all the city dwellers to work in the rice fields under the direction of the farmers. The Organization would profit handsomely on both political and economic fronts as a result, effectively killing two birds with one stone.

Politically, the Organization defeated the oppressors and elevated the social position of the previously oppressed laborers and farmers over their former bullies.

Economically, the Revolutionary Organization revamped the old unproductive system by increasing output while lowering consumption. Hence, it would be able to reap abundant economic benefits in surplus.

The political outcome after three years of this revolution, however, was a complete disaster as the Organization fell apart internally and cadres started slaying each other.

The economy failed miserably as it was unable to create any prosperity at all and only managed to starve its labor force to death.

Their failures on both scores made them realize that they needed to do something more to impress the people in order to redeem themselves. They then conceived the strange idea to attack Vietnam with China's help. When the Vietnamese resisted and the Chinese aid did not arrive on time, they scattered into hiding along the Cambodia-Thai border. To explain their defeat this time, they accused their comrades in the east of colluding with the Vietnamese. This was the self-inflicted tragedy of the Khmer Rouge.

One day, after I had finished de-worming the tobacco plants, I took out the stove to prepare porridge. At dawn the day before, the grandfather looking after the ducks had given me two fertilized duck eggs. These were invaluable for starving people like me during such a time, but it also posed a problem: how could I share this sumptuous snack with my wife and children who were at home then? My wish was highly improbable as the plantation was far away from our hut and we had no stove for cooking at home.

I also ruminated the best way to enjoy the duck eggs. After much mulling, I remembered that steamed duck egg was extremely delicious in both taste and smell. Operation Steamed Duck Eggs thus ensued. I broke the eggs into a big plate and then I sprinkled fine salt over them. Just then, I heard footsteps approaching. I looked up and found myself staring at him. I was appalled. It was none other than the cooperative chief named Dum.

His friendly voice boomed out, "Do you have anything to eat?"

I stuttered that I had two fertilized duck eggs that I had found along the dike in the rice field.

He left without saying anything. I quickly rose to escort him out respectfully and politely.

During my short conversation with Chief Dum, I had sprinkled salt on the duck eggs without paying attention to how much was added. When I returned, all the salt had dissolved into the duck eggs. I beat up the mixture a little more to ensure that the ingredients were thoroughly blended. Then I poured it into a bowl, and I put this into a pot of water for steaming before starting the fire.

Shortly after, the aroma of steamed duck eggs began to emerge and I stirred the mixture again because this tasty snack must be thoroughly cooked before its wonderful flavor can be savored. I scooped a spoonful of it into my mouth. Immediately, the burning hot sensation turned into an overwhelmingly salty, bitter taste that was difficult to swallow. The delicious taste I was craving had turned unpalatable instead!

Despite the extreme taste, it was nonetheless steamed duck eggs. I swallowed another three to four spoons of it for energy because this precious food was a blessing in those times. I gave the remaining portion to the nearby farmers who devoured it hungrily, until there was none left.

This incident with the steamed duck eggs sent chills down my spine because it was an act of betraying the cooperative. The Organization had decreed that we must be completely honest and surrender even a small snail or crab to the food store, not hide and eat it ourselves. Anyone betraying the cooperative was to receive personal responsibility (be severely punished).

I had betrayed the cooperative under the very eyelashes of its chief. Should I keep mum and wait for his reaction, or should I voluntarily declare my mistake at the group meeting? If rumors spread about this, what would befall me? What would happen to the kind grandfather taking care of the ducks, who would be implicated just because he took great pity on me?

This matter gnawed at me and bothered me for a long time, until I heard from the grandfather in charge of the plantation that the chief had no intention of bringing it up.

The Last Straw

One day, at the end of March 1978, a cruel misfortune descended on my fourth child named Yoopeer.

Yoopeer was six years old then. He and some other boys in his group were ordered to collect cow dung along the rice fields. Instead, they went hunting for field mice, which they grilled to eat before returning. Their activity enraged the spy unit chief named Pum. He ordered all those boys who had disobeyed the Organization's instruction to report for their punishment.

The inhumane punishment he imposed was to stuff each boy individually into a gunny sack, which was then tied up. Due to the lack of air inside the sacks, some boys fainted, while others were so terrified that they defecated or urinated as they tried to struggle their way out.

Yoopeer was among them. At that moment, one boy ran to the plantation to inform me about Yoopeer's predicament. I was outraged when I heard this. I grabbed my sickle, slung it on my shoulder and ran on, asking where my son was being held so that I could free him from the sack. Even if I had to put up a struggle, I had to protect my family line regardless of the consequences.

In the middle of the road, a friend intercepted me and begged me to calm down. If I were to do anything rash, bad consequences would descend upon me, my family and even extend to everyone in the cooperative. Just then, another friend came to tell me that Yoopeer had already been released from the sack and was not in danger. He had fainted quickly. As for Pum, he was taken away by the cooperative chief to be held at his house. To avoid further mishap, I returned to the plantation.

My furious outburst had taken place in full public view and did not escape the eyes of the cooperative's executive committee.

That evening, the gong announcing a meeting echoed repeatedly, a signal for us to assemble at the rice field to the north.

When we had all gathered, the executive committee proclaimed its correct method to completely liberate us from the American Empire and its allies. Below are abstracts of some speeches by the cooperative leaders who spoke at length until it was time to discuss group issues:

The Organization had destroyed the feudalists, capitalists, reactionaries, conservatives, *bourgeois* and had taken steps to study and search for the truth. It not only had the spirit to take steps but also had the spirit of the laborers and farmers, who were the masters of the whole country. Since antiquity, there had never been a time like this when laborers and farmers were elevated to become the masters of the country. The people decided to raise the laborers and farmers to this high position for the country's prosperity. Now the Organization would continue on this revolutionary path by increasing the quota to four tons of rice per hectare. If this new target was not reached, the Organization would instruct the executive committee to start stuffing people, rather than rice grains, into gunny sacks for not abiding by the revolutionary position, which would allow the revolution's enemies to penetrate deeper within. The internal enemies were the property owners, proprietors and capitalists. The external enemies were those resisting the revolution – the supporters of Imperial America and its CIA agents; or KGB agents who were revisionists of Soviet socialism.

(Such rhetoric issued forth regularly from then on. Moreover, they could make such proclamations non-stop for the whole day and night.)

After this lecture, it was the turn of one striking woman in the cooperative's leadership. She was called Chief Yan and was married to a man in the executive committee named Tan. Both husband and wife were notorious for being very vile, vicious and mean. They always interrogated the newcomers, especially those who had come from distant places, to dig up the latter's background. Whenever they saw us, they stared at us through their eyelashes like we were their former foes who were wrongly placed above them. As we came from the urban areas, they never spoke to us except to order us about as human parasites that they could crush and destroy at will. (I had encountered them previously when they called me to treat their pregnant child when my family and I first arrived at Toul Kork village.)

Suddenly, this woman called for me at the group meeting and asked, "I heard Comrade is angry with the Organization for stuffing your child inside a sack. Is this true or not?"

I replied that I was not angry with the Organization, which had liberated me from Imperial America and its allies. I just pitied my child who was stuffed into a sack until he fainted because I still had some characteristics that I could not completely eradicate, unlike the chiefs who were perfect role models.

She threatened me menacingly, saying the Organization must sieve chaff from rice grains every day to succeed in its socialist revolution, so I had better admit my mistake of getting angry with the Organization.

I responded that I had already spoken truthfully, and asked what more she could want me to say.

Chief Yan rebutted that from this alone, she could see that I was not totally honest with the Organization, which was getting stronger and stronger on its revolutionary path every day.

I sat down, still and silent.

She demanded once more that I come clean with the pure and pristine truth, but I continued to sit down mutely.

Chief Yan forced me again to give the truth.

Observing my silence, Grandfather Tao (the name of an old man) spoke up to urge me to tell my truth again with the words, "The Organization is very strong every day. Teacher, speak your truth."

As soon as Grandfather Tao had finished speaking, Chief Yan immediately squawked, "Who said the Organization is very strong?"

No answer.

The atmosphere became static and eerily quiet, raising goosebumps even on our heads.

Then Chief Yan declared the meeting closed. Grandfather Tao was summoned by her that night. We never saw him again.

I was absolutely enraged by the barbaric act that had befallen my child. I had already abandoned all my past accomplishments including honor, wealth and fortune to arrive at this hell hole where I lost even the most basic liberties and independence. All I had left were my feelings for my wife and children, which I could not erase at all. How could I explain this? My mind was filled with only one thought: I must avenge myself by fighting back.

Another thought was to wait and see if any danger would come upon my family and others.

The last thought was that the immediate course of action would be to run away and fight from the forest, because this was an opportunity to resist this evil regime and fulfill my duty as a husband, a father and a citizen, according to the perceptive advice of my father from the start.

That night, I could barely close my eyes.

Worry and anxiety about my plan to flee and the dangers that could befall me, my family, friends and relatives troubled me.

I realized that I had to steel my resolve once and for all, or be forever condemned as a cowardly man and an unfilial son.

Thanks to this insight, I made up my mind to stop respecting the unworthy but to give strength to those living in despair.

That next morning, I left earlier than usual to take the day's rice ration. The young women guarding the rice at the hospital were still asleep at this time. Whenever they let me in unaccompanied to collect the rice ration, I would take two rations, instead of the one ration per day that the Organization had authorized (one ration was one milk can). I cleaned and dried the extra rice at the plantation. I did this for three days and collected a small bag of rice. I thought that it would suffice, since I was going to flee alone. I traded the tobacco that I had hidden with the metalsmith in exchange for a very sharp sickle. I told him I needed to go and clear the forest. Two days later, my shining new sickle was ready for collection. I collected it and sharpened it further. This would be my weapon of resistance during my escape.

I prepared all the things to take with me on this journey: my late father's ashes; a sapphire ring that my friend named Tang Srang had given me in Pailin in 1973; my new sickle; a cigarette lighter; a tin water flask; a small stone Buddha statue; a belt; and a religious scarf from Phnom Tvak temple with a very effective magical inscription protecting its owner. I also had a bag of rice and another bag of herbal medicines. These were all the things I took to flee from the cooperative.

After that severe group meeting with Chief Yan, everyone inside the cooperative, especially me, felt a heaviness pressing on us from above. Each of us took care of our own tasks gloomily, dreading the day that the Organization would "sieve rice," as she had warned.

On quiet afternoons, I always climbed up to the top of the tamarind tree to look at the shadow of the Malai Hill in the west, partially hidden by the horizon. There was a Liberation Army base at this hill. I planned to reach it in a few days. I had no doubt that I would meet my old friend there, the former police chief of Poipet. I would confront this cooperative with an automatic machine gun and free the people from the death claws of Khmer Rouge. I would be part of a group of brave men highly respected and esteemed by the whole country.

I entertained at length such delirious thoughts out of feelings of vengeance from prolonged deprivation and desperation. I drowned myself in such delusions – until I pondered what would happen to my wife and children after I had left. What suffering would the Khmer Rouge inflict on them? Would I return in time to free them? If I stayed instead of fleeing, would they kill me?

The memory of Grandfather Tao came back. He did not make any mistake but had simply urged me to tell my truth, yet he was taken away never to be seen again. I realized that there was no doubt they would take my life sooner or later, especially since I was a former civil servant in the old regime. To save my own life, I had no choice but to fight back. Not to do so would mean meekly awaiting death like all the other past victims. After much deliberation, I decided the best option was to flee!

Escape

Two days later, I was at the top of the tamarind tree, my usual spot whenever I had some free time, when I noticed someone approaching the plantation where I worked from the cooperative. It was my friend, Lai. He was a close and trusted friend of mine. I descended from the tamarind tree to wait for him. He was terrified and took a long time to catch his breath.

I asked him what had happened. He narrated that the people working with him in the kitchen had accused him of sexual misconduct with a woman from Snuol Kaong village. This was a very serious offense. If the Organization believed it, he would be executed immediately. He was scared that he would be dealt with this very night so he had decided to run away this evening. Crying profusely, he begged me to join him because he could not escape alone. He was a very timid person by nature.

I thought to myself, "How can there be such a coincidence?! I have just decided to make my escape tomorrow" – the thirteenth day in the fifth month of the Khmer calendar (around March/April) during the period of the waning moon – "and now Hian Lai is asking me to flee with him this evening?!"

I believed in the almanac, which predicted that any journey made on this day would meet with supernatural obstacles and not proceed smoothly. However, the next day would be excellent for embarking on a journey. Hian Lai, however, stubbornly insisted that we leave that very evening. He believed that it was a good day – the twelfth day in the fifth lunar month during the period of waning moon (5 April 1978) – because he had dreamt of a cow (a good omen) the night before.

I kept quiet and did not argue further with him. During those times, it was better to play one's cards close to one's chest and prepare thoroughly before doing anything. In my heart, I had decided to run away with Hian Lai that evening.

I told him to return to his work place and prohibited him from going home to his family. We would meet at six that evening inside the small cave temple named Kork Pradak. With that, we separated.

Hian Lai left the plantation. I went to the house of Puk Kim, a Cambodian with a Laotian wife. I addressed him as "Puk" (Khmer, meaning "Father") because it was the practice to address old people this way during the Khmer Rouge regime. Old women were addressed as "May" or "Mak," meaning "Mother."

Before the revolution, Puk Kim had done odd jobs in the dense low forest frequently flooded during the rainy season called Roniem Daun Sam. He was a frank and friendly, straightforward old man with a big heart who disliked hypocrisy. I treated him as my relative inside the cooperative.

When I reached his hut, I saw him alone inside. I told him about my plan for that evening. I had come to bid him farewell and to ask for his compass because, as an ex-forester, he would surely have one. He told me to wait for his daughter, Chanthy to return from her forced labor as she had buried the compass to hide it from the Khmer Rouge. (Chanthy was a widow who was very pretty as a child. She regarded me like her own brother.)

At that very moment, Chanthy returned. Puk Kim whispered to her to dig out the compass for me. She went behind the house and returned a little while later with the compass. She gave it to me with tears streaming down her face and said, "Brother! For you as requested. It's yours already. If Brother should meet any unfavorable situation, please Brother, do not say that this is from me." I promised not to do so. I clasped her hands tenderly to bid farewell and left straight for my own house, which was not far away.

This dilapidated hut, which I had built with my own hands, had a roof and wooden planks for its floor but no walls. I had taken some very old gunny sacks to sew into curtains to act as walls. This gave us a unique advantage because from inside the house, we could see whatever was happening outside, but it was not possible for someone outside to see what was going on inside the house. I had gathered the old planks discarded by the other villagers to make the base of this four-by-four meters hut. The floor was raised about seventy centimeters above ground level to make it difficult for the spies to eavesdrop on us.

My hut was quiet. Seeing it made me nostalgic, thinking that from this evening onwards, I would leave it and all its inhabitants permanently. I lifted the curtains to see what else I should take with me and what to leave for my family's use. After looking through the things, I put them back in their usual places. Then I went to the worksite to take the pail and filled up my family's water jar.

When I was done, I saw Puk Kim approaching me. He said softly that he could not let me enter the forest by myself as I knew nothing about it. He offered to guide me because he was old already and did not have any more cares. He would lead the way in the forest for us to go and fight heroically. If he were to die, he would die without regret. I was elated to hear this and saluted him by lifting high both my hands in the traditional Khmer way.

We agreed to meet again in slightly more than one hour at the cave temple and set off with Hian Lai from there.

Puk Kim returned to his house.

I walked straight to the cow shed to take my two beloved youngest children, Voly and Jati, who were being cared for by the grandmothers in front of our house (grandmothers were old women in the cooperative who helped to look after the young children while their mothers worked). I thanked them for treating both my children well and asked them to continue doing so. Then I said goodbye and left with my kids. My wife would return shortly from her forced labor.

I made good use of this time to hug both my children for the last time. I showered both of them and changed their clothes. I reminded Jati to look after his youngest sister, Voly until their mother's return. Then I bade them farewell and departed with so much sorrow in my heart that I could barely breathe.

Oh! Pity on my children, from the youngest to the oldest! Soon, they would not have a father to guide them, but how could they thrive under the present circumstances, and what of their future?

I had to leave before my wife's return to avoid wavering from my decision when I saw her.

I went a little earlier to the Kork Pradak cave temple before my two friends. I decided to enter the bottom of the cave to rearrange my things by wrapping them in a *krama*, which I then tied with my belt to prevent them from dropping out and becoming lost during the journey.

Then I took three thin dried twigs from a small common plant to replace incense sticks and prayed. I prayed for a smooth journey to the border so that I could later return to free my country and religion from the vicious claws of these savages. If not, I asked to die inside the forest. I gave thanks that this cave temple was well taken care of and also thanked my parents for always looking after me.

My heart at that time was heavy and full of despair because I had lost all liberties and all hopes for myself, my country and its future. I regretted intensely my decision not to leave my country at the very beginning because of my excessively nationalist and socialist allegiance. (Between 17 and 19 April 1975, Khmers were free to go live in Thailand, because the Khmer Rouge had not arrived yet. From my house to the border, the distance was less than four kilometers.)

After this, I exited the cave to meet Puk Kim and Hian Lai who were already waiting impatiently at the entrance of the cave temple.

When it became dark enough, we headed directly west. Puk Kim led the way and we simply followed him. As I walked, I reached down to feel for the Buddha statue that I had taken along with me to ensure a smooth journey, but it was gone. I guessed I had misplaced it inside the cave. Perhaps the Buddha did not agree with our plan to embark on this flight to freedom? It soon became pitch dark and we could not see the road. We felt our way through and lifted our legs high to avoid tripping.

About two hours later, it seemed like we had reached a village. I whispered to ask Puk Kim if we had reached some place. He replied that it was perhaps Plov Damrei village near Lvea village. A moment later, Puk Kim walked straight into the wall of a hut, and we heard the sounds of breaking twigs. He quickly retreated to grab both of us and we sprinted. At that instant, I heard a sound inside the hut shouting, "Who is it?" We did not reply as we were panic-stricken and did not know the code words that would permit us to carry on with our journey.

One moment later, the gong for making public announcements pealed persistently near us. In the dark, we saw bright fire torches darting here and there looking for us.

My two mates held each other tightly out of fear, bewilderment and panic. I saw their fright, so I told them, "Please, Puk Kim and Hian, don't be afraid. Come and stand behind me. Face me and memorize by heart this prayer to hide ourselves."

They got my message and immediately rushed to stand behind me. My sickle was placed directly at my feet. We were beneath a big hardwood tree often used in construction and I was afraid that some branches would fall on us if the fire torches came too close. I started to chant the prayer at times audibly and at times inaudibly because I could not remember it clearly. I prayed that Puk Kim and Hian Lai would trust me and not be scared of their own shadows after deciding to flee together. After this, I recited another prayer, but I could not remember this one completely either.

I learn the importance of memorizing prayers from this experience because during emergencies, our minds can go blank from panic or bewilderment and we end up not knowing what to do. At such times, chanting prayers is an effective tool to calm our minds down.

I had resolved that if they approached us, we would fight with the sickle and not be deterred. Luckily, the fire torches went past us without coming near at all. Suddenly, the sounds of three or four barking dogs headed straight towards us. I rued that I had not learnt the chant to tie a dog's mouth, which I had seen in my teacher's book. The dogs came in front of us but miraculously left to follow the torch bearers.

All three of us were relieved and started to breathe again. We quickly ran out from behind the big tree towards the west again.

About fifty meters away, we ran into some people sleeping in the middle of a field. Someone shouted, "Who stepped on me?"

I replied, "Sorry, I didn't see you."

We hastily ran into the forest until we reached a small overflowing river. Luckily, we could all swim and could use the tin water flask as a float too. Reaching the other shore, we filled it to the brim with water and prodded on.

I was completely exhausted from the cold water. My whole body was covered in white goosebumps and my heart had turned into stone. We walked a little farther until we came to a big plot of land that had just been plowed with a tractor. We trekked across it with great difficulty because each step caused our feet to sink into the mud. I pounded my legs and buttocks but could not move any faster. We saw fire torches belonging to the unit plowing the land using a tractor darting in the distance. That unit worked the whole night without rest. I told Puk Kim, "Puk! I cannot walk any farther. Please Puk, head straight towards the forest."

Puk led us towards the left and told us that straight ahead was a village named Damnak Preah Ang, near to Anlong Somnor village.

It was almost daybreak when we spotted some pale-colored forest ants in front of us. A little hope arose in me on seeing the forest. My legs were no longer at my command because my joints, muscles and buttocks had all stopped working. I sought my companions' help to drag me into the forest. Puk Kim and Hian Lai supported me to walk into the forest. Both of them were also fatigued because we had walked with all of our might for one whole night. When they put me down, my legs felt a little better. Sunlight scattered across the horizon. We had gone far enough into the forest. This was our good luck, because if we had not entered the forest by daybreak, we would surely be seen. Now that we had the forest to shield us, we were not so worried. We could hide and rest quietly. We drank half of the water in the tin flask. We had only about two liters of water left. We searched for a secluded spot to rest.

From afar, we could hear the sounds of logging and people speaking indistinctly. Near us, a troop of monkeys were noisily swinging from tree to tree high above us. We slept here and the primates soon left us.

Suddenly I heard sharp sounds from above that startled me. It sounded like the ghost in the movies, "...Hooo... Hooo..." I searched for the mysterious caller in vain. What was it?

Puk Kim told me to ignore it. The sounds came from a species of small bird called *m'dye s'ngun*.

We heard it throughout the day. In the evening, we had no food except some water, which we sipped to relieve our throats. The dried rice we had was no help because it was sticky and stuck to our mouths. We could neither chew nor swallow it. We needed to find water quickly but we did not know where the nearest water source was.

By evening, the sounds of logging and conversation stopped completely. Immediately, we came out of hiding to continue our journey. We had to walk in the open again this night and were worried that we would run into Khmer Rouge soldiers. We did not walk quickly like the previous night because we were exhausted. Hian Lai and I could not tell the direction at all so we simply followed Puk Kim. If he jumped over a mound, we followed suit. Sometimes, we came across obstacles such as sharp stakes made from bamboo, metal or wood. These were stuck densely into the ground.

We started to miss our steps. Puk Kim was a wise guide inside the forest. He knew beforehand the places where there were such sharp stakes, even in dark and obscure places. He told us that we had run across a real minefield – we had reached the old Khmer Rouge base where there would definitely be many such booby traps. We tiptoed around these, unable to put down our heels at all. We had to be ultra-careful to skirt around these stakes in this plantation approximately forty meters long. We were scared stiff as we could not see them in the dark.

At dawn, Puk Kim said we had reached an abandoned village called Jai Mong. The Khmer Rouge had evacuated all the villagers to live in a cooperative. We drank some of the remaining water. Puk Kim led us to a natural pond formerly used by the villagers. We folded our *kramas* and dipped one end into the muddy water. Then we sucked the water from the other end of our *kramas* to fill our stomachs.

We continued our journey wearily. From this time onwards, we walked all day and night if we could because we were now far from the presence of people. We came to a mangrove forest and Puk Kim led us along a small creek to avoid a detour through the tall forest trees. At the same time, we were worried that the creek would be flooded. We walked from dawn till dusk on the meandering road that ran along the creek but there was not a single drop of water. Puk Kim said that in the past, this creek had never been dry. Now, even the potholes that used to collect water were arid. He said if we were to continue this way, we would soon die from thirst. The alternative was to backtrack and search for flowing water along that old farming village.

I had complete confidence in Puk Kim. He was our leader, so we retraced our steps.

When dawn broke, we left the forest and walked on the left side of a field, fearful of running into any villagers who might have evaded the evacuation. We were thoroughly exhausted.

I was shocked to observe the skeletal and sickly physiques of my companions. We had only been gone three nights, but their life energy had completely dissipated. Hollow eyes, sunken cheeks, dry mouths, cracked lips. On their bodies, hands and legs, only skin remained, covering bones that were jutting out. All their flesh had melted away because of their sheer terror of the possible dangers ahead. Would we have the good fortune to survive this perilous plight?

Near the forest edge, we saw a small thatched hut, suggesting people were living here. Puk Kim and Hian Lai whispered to me to ask for water from them. Both of them would hide in the forest first. I moved ahead in a daze, dizzy and sleepy. About ten meters from the hut, I halted because I fell asleep standing. Shortly after, I succumbed and plonked myself down to sleep on the ground. Hian Lai came to drag me up and pushed me towards the hut again. I felt much better after that momentary respite and went to the hut. It was empty.

I returned to my companions and we decided to search for water behind the forest trees. We rested for a short while and then quickly set off again to look for water. We were now clear-headed and had more energy and would not let drowsiness overcome us again. We knew clearly that it was time to nourish our bodies, but we had no food at all. We could not swallow anything without water. I chewed the shoots of the Malay rose apple (also known as otaheite or *jambu*) plant. However, its sap glued my tongue and palate together, obstructing my breathing. I quickly spat it out and used my fingers to clear any remaining leaves out from my mouth.

We could not find any water left behind by the former villagers. We could not find any food either to substitute for water. All we asked for now was to find water to replace food to save our lives. Humans can live without food for three weeks, but cannot survive without water for more than three days.

We searched for water by surveying our surroundings for any fresh green succulent plants growing together. We walked from one brushwood field to another and unexpectedly came across a well in the shape of a small pond. There was a little water at the bottom. We drew water from the well by lowering the pail into the mud and then hauling it up. We managed to collect slightly more than half a pail of water before the well dried up. We wiped the mud from the pail and kept some of the water for later use.

We also found some uneven stone surfaces with water accumulated on them. We sucked water from them using our *kramas*, in the same way we had drunk earlier at Jai Mong village.

We were happy to have water to drink even though we were so fatigued that we had lost all our fighting spirit. Our eyes started playing tricks on us, causing us to walk unsteadily. Our ears buzzed and our mouths were bitter and dry. We pressed on sluggishly but knew clearly that death was near. We wished only for rain.

Shouts of strange animals came from high above our heads. We did not bother with the compass anymore. We were obsessed with water. Where water could be found, we headed straight for it.

Samsaric Suffering

It was only at dawn on the fifth day of our escape that we found some water in the forest with many hanging vines. We cut these and put them into our mouths so that the water in them would trickle down our throats. No water flowed out if we yanked these vines into our hands. We satisfied our thirst in this way and also relieved our hunger by munching on them. They were delicious.

We did not feel so exhausted that morning. We prodded on silently. Around four in the late afternoon, I could not continue walking anymore. I was absolutely spent. I asked my mates to stop for a rest. I thought inside my heart that I would soon die. I begged Puk Kim and Hian Lai to let me die and push on without me. If they waited for me, they would lose time and it could also jeopardize their lives. If they encountered the Khmer Rouge soldiers, their suffering would double.

Both of them disagreed with me and implored me not to give up. They told me to endure a little longer because the divine beings would come to our rescue soon. They supported me to enter a place hidden in the forest. One hour later, all my remaining energy left me and I could not even sit up. I collapsed onto the ground and lost all consciousness.

I did not know how long I lay unconscious there. I only recalled that it was afternoon when I passed out. When I woke up, I searched for my things only to find that my sickle and compass were missing. I thought that I could not go far without these items to cut the vegetation and to tell the direction. I lay there quietly for a while, listening to the sound of raindrops falling on the leaves. I looked up and saw a huge turkey-like wild bird with black wings and a big crest. A flaccid, dark red fold of skin was hanging from under its beak till its neck. When it saw me, it squawked "kluk, kluk" and flew into the forest.

I went back to sleep.

Shortly after, I heard the sounds of falling rain on stone. The sounds became increasingly stronger and heavier. I thought they sounded like human footsteps. I hid myself behind the thick vegetation and peeked. I saw two pairs of legs which I instantly recognized. Puk Kim and Hian Lai!

I rubbed my eyes to confirm before calling out to them, delighted.

"Puk Kim! Puk Kim!"

My friends stared at me stumped and then they chorused, "Teacher!"

I got up and threw myself forward to hug them with overwhelming happiness.

Puk Kim exclaimed trembling, "What happened?"

Hian Lai also did not understand why I was here.

Hian Lai asked me, "Teacher told me last night that you quit, so how come you caught up with us?"

I replied, "I was too weary to walk anymore. I just woke up a little before this!"

My two friends stared at one another and chimed, "We lost our way for one day and one night!"

Hian Lai poured some water from the tin flask and divided it equally among us. It was water from the hanging vines.

Some hope returned to my heart because I had slept for forty-eight hours and had recovered some energy. We headed west according to the compass. In the evening, we unexpectedly saw a luxurious bunch of climbing vines. We stuffed ourselves with water by drinking numerous times. That night, we slept in the forest.

The next morning, the sun was up by the time we woke up. We doggedly dragged ourselves on. Soon after, we reached a bamboo forest. All the bamboos had died and were completely dry and white in color. We walked timidly along its fringe, trampling on clumps of the dead bamboos. The heat from the sun scorched our skin and caused us much suffering. Our eyes were completely dry. Our mouths were dehydrated like paper. Our parched throats had no saliva at all.

We reached a canal that had a tree with enough canopy to provide some shade. We stopped here to rest on the ground. I felt the soil with my hands. It was dry, but the earth on my back appeared to have some humidity, which refreshed me somewhat. Hian Lai was groaning in agony. I muttered hoarsely that each of us escaped to flee from death but now we were battling death in the middle of the forest. We could not run anymore. We must receive our karma, the consequences of our decisions.

My body was feverish. I felt intolerably hot all over. I was dehydrated and cried out loudly but could not describe what I felt. I thought, "If the Khmer Rouge offered me a glass of water in exchange for my life now, I would willingly barter with them."

I had trouble speaking and was too parched to talk, so I challenged myself mentally by recalling my children's names according to their birth sequence. I remembered six of them but could not recall Yoopeer's name at all. My memory was otherwise intact.

I checked my pulse and found only a light trembling. I knew clearly that death had already entered my body. I was not afraid of dying because I made good use of this time to study it. I was completely convinced of my own imminent demise. Suddenly, I had the sensation of a millipede crawling on me. It crawled from my neck to my cheek, then near my eye and ate my eye rheum (in Khmer, it is called "eye shit"). I did not have strength to pick it off. After eating all the eye discharge from one eye, it left.

My body started to change after this. My eyes, which had been dry until then, became practically blind. My ears started to hear slow, repeated, irregular thumps with buzzing sounds. My body changed from numb, sluggish and slow to completely unfeeling. I put my hand on my body but I had no sensation.

Curiously, I felt better because my thirst and fever diminished considerably. I was certain that Death had come to take me.

I shouted the names of my native village, my parents and my wife to the deities, saying, "I'm going to die this time. Please divine beings and guardian angels, let all these people know. Please also recall that I had done many good deeds, such as giving alms to monks; observing Buddhist ceremonies and dedicating the merits to ancestors and patrons; treating poor people free of charge; and donating to those in need. My father told me before his death that I would not perish prematurely because I had accumulated many merits."

After making this declaration (I could not remember if I had said it aloud or silently), I started chanting prayers in my heart.

I did not know how long I prayed. Suddenly, I felt the earth shaking and heard sounds like thunder rumbling. People were shouting, crying or wailing out their regret and mental anguish. Some were laughing derisively after hurting others' feelings or injuring them. I tried to figure out what was going on. Just then, a black shadow in the shape of a human form flashed before me. It melted into the distance until it was the size of a bean. My chest was congested and I felt sick. Then I fainted.

I had no idea how long it was before I regained consciousness. This time, a similar event happened but it was shorter in duration. I was freezing cold. I began to regain some bodily sensations. It was as if I had woken up from a very long slumber. I asked myself where I was and what had happened. I felt thirsty again but was not agitated like before.

My eyes started to perceive a little again. I felt for my hands, legs and then my whole body. I sat up and then stood up. The vegetation around me was wet and radiant. Water was dripping from the leaves. My *krama* and clothes were wet. The ground was wet, but there were no puddles.

I sucked the water from my *krama*. I also sucked the red scarf with protective religious inscription written in black ink. I drank thus until they became dry. Then I took them to wipe the raindrops on the leaves and drank again. The scarf had discolored and parts of the inscription were lost by now. After relieving my thirst in this way, I regained some energy and my body felt cool and comfortable. I stumbled towards my companions who were sleeping some five meters away from me. (When we are fatigued, we tend to misjudge distance as farther than it actually is.)

The most horrendous and heart-wrenching sight greeted me.

Puk Kim was dead stiff, in a state of *rigor mortis*. He was facing up with his limbs bent wildly as if he had struggled before dying. I knelt beside his body and paid my last and highest respect to him with great grief in my heart. He was a good man with a kind heart who had lost his life to help me. His generosity and goodwill towards me were immeasurable. How could I ever repay his good deed? I am a staunch Buddhist and dedicate the merits of all my virtues to his soul. May his soul rest peacefully in paradise.

(I heard that his daughter, Chanthy is living in Canada today.)

About three meters away from Puk Kim's corpse, Hian Lai lay spread-eagled on the ground, sleeping quietly. ("Hian" means "elder brother" in the Chinese dialect, Teochew. I always addressed him as "Hian" even though he was younger than me.) I shook him to wake him up. His body appeared to have a little warmth but he could not be roused. I wrung a wet *krama* to quench his thirst but the water simply flowed out of his mouth.

I broke down. However, crying my heart out to express my grief and pain could not revive them. Worse still, I was dangling from the cliff of death myself.

I was utterly devastated. I plopped myself down onto the ground like a stone. However, I resolved to fight on valiantly and not let a bad situation defeat me, just like my father who had struggled hard all his life since birth. Even if I were to die with the next step I took, I would press on and not let death claim our lives without putting up a heroic fight.

Fatigue lured me to sleep but I staggered on. After about ten meters, I folded down to sleep.

When I felt stronger, I continued on my journey. A few days later, I noticed that the animal that I had heard making a laughing sound almost every day had stopped its mocking suddenly.

It was my good fortune that the rain started to fall. It fell practically every day, flooding the Roniem Daun Sam Forest and Malai Hill, but the raindrops were small and the duration short. Nonetheless, even though it was not torrential, it made the atmosphere cool and humid, so my journey became more bearable.

After each rainfall, I licked the raindrops on the leaves to quench my thirst. With bamboos, I could obtain more water where their sheaths flaked off above the soil than from licking their leaves. No puddles formed on the ground.

The raindrops quenched my thirst even though I had no food.

I walked alone in the forest in this manner, just like in the legends. When night fell, I had no choice as to where I was, but I had no fear either. Besides populated areas and hunger, no other enemy threatened me anymore.

I loved exploring the deserted mountain forest with its irregular and uneven terrain. Here was a shallow river with a bamboo forest next to it. There was a spacious field of long reed. There were ants, birds and wild animals. There were all kinds of vines – creeping, climbing and interweaving from one tree to another. Some looked like snakes, others like rope or plaits. There were also big and small vines that could be used to make furniture, to decorate homes or to make the small round rice baskets that we used to eat from.

I was happy whenever I chanced upon succulent vines because it was a type of special food that sustained me. Normally, I would not have dared to venture up the small hill, but I loved to explore its forest and the large rocks, so I ended up walking a little farther each time. I ascended to the midpoint of the hill and sat down on a stone. I asked the divine beings to send me some edible fruits, leaves or vines – in fact anything at all that could be eaten, whether leaves, flowers or fruits.

As soon as I had uttered these words, I unexpectedly noticed a plant in a crevice between the rocks. I did not know its name but its fruit was the size of four Jambolan plums and had a delicious, juicy taste. I was still hungry, so I fingered around in case I could find something else to eat. I edged forward and even found cereal grains mixed with the soil and some unripe seeds. Not far from me, I saw a small green immature vine about ten centimeters long hanging from the moss on the rock. I nibbled on it. It tasted like a species of edible vine. My prayer was answered even though it was too little to satisfy my hunger pangs.

About fifty meters away, a young tiger emerged from the forest but it quickly slithered back when it spotted me. I lay on the rock, observing the flora above me. There is a species of vine with ends that look like python snakes. When the wind blows, these ends sway like pythons moving their heads. I had heard from the elders that this species of vine deep inside the forest is aptly named "Python Vine." It is so tough and leathery that it cannot be severed with a knife or even an ax. Only those medicine men who know a secret chant to soften it can cut it by reciting the chant. They use it to make a potion that endows those who drink it with impenetrable tough skin. However, I did not have the energy to test this theory at that time.

It was now day ten of my escape. I dragged myself doggedly towards the west. I reached another mountain on this day. I ascended it with great difficulty and misery because there was no ready path. In the afternoon, at the back of the mountain, I chanced upon a one-meter-tall zinc water barrel. I uncapped it to let the water out, but there was not a single drop. Feeling despondently that there was no water inside, I tried to peep through the cap into the barrel. There was some water at the bottom. I wrapped the cap opening with my mouth and began to suck air into my lungs. Instantly, there was a sound like two empty containers striking one another and water gushed out. I quickly gulped down the water to alleviate my thirst, full of happiness and hope.

Having fully satisfied my thirst, I lay down to rest. Water continued spurting out till the barrel ran dry. I felt energized as if I had received blessed water from heaven. The water tasted strange. It alleviated my thirst completely but made me crave meat. I blurted out to the forest fairies to bestow on me a turtle for food. I had barely finished speaking when my left foot slipped into a hole with sharp bamboo stakes, piercing the sole of my foot into my ankle. Blood squirted out. Instinctively, my right leg moved forward and got caught in another booby trap. Sharp pains shot up as the pointed bamboo stakes cut into my right calf. Now both my legs were injured and I was trapped in these holes. I considered pulling both legs out but worried about what to do if my blood would not stop flowing. I got myself together in order not to panic and thought that I would need to look for some food to avoid dying from starvation in this state. Just then, I heard the sounds of people chatting from behind the mountain. I was relieved, thinking that help was on my way and I would soon be freed. I waited quietly for their arrival but as they approached, I heard them singing the revolutionary songs of the Khmer Rouge.

My hope was dashed and in my panic, I yanked both legs out from the holes, completely seized with alarm at what would happen next. Two Khmer Rouge soldiers peered through the forest and came closer to the scene of my mishap. I had turned face down pretending to be dead, but my mouth was silently chanting a mantra I had known by heart to obscure their vision, "Buddha, cover their eyes. Dharma, cover their eyes. Sangha, cover their eyes." Even as I muttered this under my breath, I was afraid that they would approach to confirm I was really dead by slashing my body.

An instant passed. The song of the soldiers in black faded from my ears. My chant worked! Perhaps my guardian angel was watching over me to shroud me from their sight? Maybe they were just too lazy or careless to simply assume that they had seen my corpse? The soldiers ascended the mountain and left.

I picked myself up quickly. Blood had tainted the soil deep red. I looked at the traps that I had slipped into. They had dug the holes and covered them with thatch.

Inside one hole, there were five to six bamboo stakes. Three of these were about one meter long each. Such stakes could kill a human or an animal falling on them. There were also shorter stakes, perhaps thirty to forty centimeters, inside the shallower holes. These were not as deadly and were more numerous. I searched for a way to cross over to the other side of the mountain without leaving a trail of blood for the Khmer Rouge soldiers to trace me. Shuffling along on my buttocks, I moved slowly along the edge of the booby traps to descend the mountain slope, perhaps for fifty meters. Then I ascended the mountain again and grabbed the leaves of the vegetation around me to erase the blood blots. After that, I masticated the leaves of a small common plant which I then applied on my wounds. I tore my *krama* into small strips to bandage my wounds. The bleeding soon stopped but I had lost much blood. I replaced the bandages with new ones before pushing on my butt to descend the mountain slope on the other side. I would have to move like this until my wounds healed.

I had come under new physical danger on top of having to cope with starvation, thirst, exhaustion and the capricious weather. It had been ten days since I last had proper food. What vindictiveness or malice had caused me to receive such torture? Was it because I had hunted small animals like crabs, frogs and others to eat in my adolescence? Had this been my destiny since birth? Or was it retribution from some past lives? Even if I had erred previously, surely my suffering now would negate all my past misdeeds? When and how would this ordeal to repay my karmic debts end?

My painful journey on my buttocks was like a turtle's crawl. My maximum speed was perhaps one kilometer a day. My initial plan was to enter the forest where I would join a liberation army to wrest my country back from the Khmer Rouge brutes. Now I was fighting Death himself.

When my two hapless friends, Puk Kim and Hian Lai passed away, leaving me all alone, I had vowed to push on no matter how difficult the journey ahead might be. What was I living for if not to defend my country and religion? I would stand by the pledge I had made at the ancient temple when I was ordered to destroy it.

I pushed along on my backside into the forest all night and all day. I inched forward even when half-asleep. I had no schedule except to keep going. Food came from tree scraps or fallen fruits on the ground. Water came from dew and raindrops that had collected on the leaves. Any day without rain was a day of reckoning for me. Even though rain fell every day, it was not enough to make even a small puddle.

One day, I came to a field with closely spaced trees. I stared at the azure blue sky and thought that there was no hope for rain as it was already afternoon. I shouted to the divine beings to send some rain before evening or I would surely die.

Just then, I felt something behind me. I reached back to see what it was and was most astonished to find two fruits. Each fruit was pale yellow and round. I did not know what they were but I was so famished that I was prepared to eat anything. However, I dared not chomp down immediately. I took a small bite first to check for any adverse reaction. It was delicious with a sweet taste. The juice was sticky and stuck to my teeth. A moment later, I bit off another piece and chewed it. I swallowed this piece and waited a while to confirm that it was safe to eat. I waited for perhaps another fifteen minutes. Nothing happened so I ate both of them. The fruit was like a guava fruit externally and a fibrous gourd internally. Its flesh tasted like an overripe apple. This was my first meal since I had escaped from the cooperative – a fruit I had never before seen with a delicious taste. Strangely, I did not see the tree it came from nearby. It must have either been my good luck or divine intervention.

I continued my way painstakingly like a turtle to cut across the brushwood. In the evening, I saw many fallen ripe red fruits covering the ground. Each fruit was the size of a thumb and its tree was as tall as a tamarind tree. I took one to taste. It was bittersweet. I sat gazing at the many small insects flying erratically above the fruits. Some animals had bitten the ripe fruits but none had eaten them. I had previously heard from the elders that before eating any unknown fruit in the forest, one should first observe the animals. If the animals ate it, then it should be safe for human consumption. However, if the animals did not eat it, then one should not eat it as it was probably poisonous. According to this advice, I dared not eat these fruits even though they looked very appetizing.

My legs were swollen, threatening to burst and shooting intermittent pains. I continued wearily on, waking and sleeping, held only by the steadfast goal to cover one kilometer a day. From my present location, it was another two to three kilometers to the Thai border. I was constantly looking out for water because the rainfall was insufficient. Sometimes, I saw butterflies grouped together on the ground like flowers. I assumed they were full of water so I had caught one and squeezed it like a flower petal to extract some water. There was no water at all. Perhaps there was moisture on the ground that the butterflies had come to absorb to quench their own thirst.

The next day, I reached the virgin forest. I could obtain water from the vines in a forest like this. However, if the vines grew high beyond the reach of my hands, I could not drink from them. Another difficulty was the lack of a ready path, which made it hard for me to make my way, shuffling on my posterior. I figured that I had no choice but to go around rather than to cut straight through the forest. Anyway, I was too exhausted, so I napped to recover my strength. I lost track of how long I slept. When I woke up, I was astonished to see many quadruped hoof prints around me. The animals had beaten a path through the forest while I was asleep. I was truly amazed. There were at least ten of them trampling past me, yet I was not woken up by them? The animals were most helpful as they had cut a path for me through the thick forest.

I continued on my bum along the track made by these animals. I knew that they had gone in search of a water hole they frequented. The beasts and I shared the same purpose – to get drinking water.

I noticed that among the hoof prints, the bigger ones resembled buffalo hooves and the smaller ones their calves'. However, these were not domesticated but wild bovines. It was a pleasant surprise for me because I had assumed that these years of civil war had decimated all the forest animals. I was happy that some, not least these wild buffaloes, had survived. I no longer worried about how to navigate through the forest because these wild creatures had cut a path for me.

On the fourteenth day, I reached a wide spacious field full of grass and small shrubs but without a single tree. This field was around one kilometer wide, which posed a challenge for me.

It reminded me of an incident just before the *coup d'etat* orchestrated by the Americans to overthrow Samdech Norodom Sihanouk. (I can only remember the gist of this story, and not very clearly.)

Just before the *coup*, a group of Khmer Serei had captured a Thai soldier and a Thai log trader with some military supplies, including a small aircraft, to deliver to the Royal Khmer army. I heard that the Khmer Serei chief allowed the Thais to construct an airfield near the Cambodia-Thai border. I therefore assumed that the flat open field before me was this airfield at the former Khmer Serei region of Trat Tra.

I dared not cross this field because I reckoned it would take me the whole day. To cross a wide open field in broad daylight was too risky because there would surely be many Khmer Rouge soldiers near the border.

Initially, I edged my way slowly along the forest fringe, planning to wait till nightfall to attempt my way out. Just then I saw, about thirty meters away, a female wild bovine with her calf feeding on the grass in the middle of the field.

The mother had big, strong horns. Its body was black from its neck to its chest. Its four legs were white from the knees to the ankles. I thought that whatever animal it was (Could it be the *kouprey*? The *kouprey* is Cambodia's elusive national animal, widely believed to be extinct now), it would surely be aggressive out of its motherly instinct to protect its young. However, their presence made me realize that there were no Khmer Rouge soldiers around. I decided right then to transverse the field.

Time was as precious as my life. From one day to another, my weakened body had labored on resolutely, despite my leg injuries. My legs were swollen and emitting sharp pains periodically. I could not delay any longer.

I gingerly pushed myself forward directly towards the animals. The mother appeared to understand my intention and allowed me to pass, even escorting me. As I inched my way painfully forward, it also advanced, leading its calf with it, but otherwise, both were quite indifferent to my presence. By evening, I had successfully crossed to the other side. The mother-and-child pair entered the forest and disappeared.

I also entered the forest to rest. That night, I observed sounds of running footsteps and explosions above me from the forest behind. The commotion only stopped in the morning. I pushed forward on my buttocks again, having recovered some energy from last night's rest. Along the trodden track, I saw the broken branch of a big tree lying on the ground. I understood immediately that the Khmer Rouge and Thai armies had exchanged fire the night before.

I realized that I was already near the Khmer-Thai border already. My despair increased. Before I left on this journey, I had been determined to flee into the forest and fight against the Khmer Rouge from there.

Now that I had reached the border, however, I had no choice but to cross over into Thailand.

I thought this made me a coward who had fled by himself and left his wife and children to receive punishment in his place. However, I could not bear to continue suffering in the cooperative, waiting for death. Another thought was to go to Thailand and get my wounds treated first. Plus, I needed to find some food to replenish my energy before looking for a strategy to defeat the Khmer Rouge.

In 1975, my family and I had lived in the Nimet community, around six kilometers from Poipet. I had good connections at a border town named Aranya (in Thai: Aranyaprathet) and hoped that the pharmacists there would sympathize with my predicament and help me.

On the fifteenth day of my journey –it was 20 April 1978 – I was making my way as usual, pushing on my buttocks along the track made by the animals. It had been a dusty morning. Suddenly rain poured down heavily and strong winds swept about wildly, shaking the whole forest. I sheltered quietly under a shady tree. My body was freezing and trembling, but it was different from before. Since I had embarked on this trip, this was the first time that I had encountered weather like this. The sky sprayed rain on the vegetation and made roaring sounds throughout the forest.

I spread my *krama* and the scarf with religious inscription on the ground to collect water so as to quench my thirst. I did this until I was full. It had rained only a little each day for many days, never heavily like today. When the rain stopped, I continued my journey.

Along my way, I vaguely heard the sounds of frogs bellowing. Nature has its own rhythm. Small forest crabs left their holes in great numbers, carpeting the forest floor. (Inside the Roniem Daun Sam Forest, there is a species of crab smaller than the paddy crabs but with longer legs. It has very quick reflexes. If it pinches a person, it will not release until its pincer is cut off.) I caught these crabs to suck for nutrients but they did not taste good.

I pushed on until the evening. I reached the edge of a thick forest where reed, areca palms, sugar canes and other small plants grew densely together. Rain had just fallen and the grass was lush with water flowing over it. The water was muddy and some plants that had earlier bowed from the onslaught of the rain were now straightening. On a road to the north, I saw fresh human footprints.

I was afraid. I thought these must belong to Khmer Rouge soldiers. Then I noticed that the footprints had entered the space where I was, reversed direction and gone another way towards a path across the dense forest another ten meters or so. I hurriedly crawled towards it. Through the gaps of the vegetation, I saw an opening about the height of a crouching adult.

I took a risk and entered that small tunnel, since I had no choice anyway. Due to the dense canopy above, the path was dark and obscure. There were footprints of people walking to and fro. I pushed on with all my might because this was a dangerous place. Not long after, I saw flickering lights flashing at the other end. When I reached the end of the tunnel, I saw a big tree serving as a bridge to cross a stream. This stream was almost a small river and had water flowing slowly at its bottom. I pushed my way across this improvised bridge. By the time I reached the other side, it was night.

I saw a steep hill before me and on the plateau, there were fruit trees. It looked like a plantation or farm. Banana plants, jackfruit trees and coconut trees were left smoldering after having been burned. There were no houses. I was sure that I was on Thai territory.

The stream that I had just crossed must have been the border demarcation between Cambodia and Thailand. My heart was fearful and overwhelmed by confusing emotions. Tears welled up and flowed uncontrollably as I yearned for my homeland, my wife and children, my mother and siblings. I remembered my vow in April 1975 that I would not run away from my birth place when friends entreated me to leave for Thailand. I had betrayed their trust because I did not keep my word.

What should I do now that I was in Thailand?

I paid my respect and reported to the deities watching over Cambodians and especially the spirits guarding the forest fauna and flora that I did not forget my promise. I did not wish to abandon my motherland but circumstances compelled me on this course of action. I asked for the ten transcendent virtues from the Buddha: generosity/alms giving; morality; transcendence over the material world/renunciation; wisdom; forbearance; vigor; truthfulness; resolve; loving kindness; and equanimity. I prayed that my spiritual master would watch over me so that I would have the strength, influence and courage to persevere with my goal and not give up because of obstacles along the way.

After praying, I turned towards Cambodian territory to pay my last respects and to bid farewell to my people and native land, unable to suppress the longing and melancholy that had welled up inside me. If I lived, I would return to exterminate the Khmer Rouge without fail.

I prayed for a long time. The moon was full and luminous that night. It illuminated the forest brightly like the morning sun.

I was starving and decided to chop a small banana plant to suck water from it. I plunged my knife into the middle of a banana plant but it got stuck. I rested to recover my breath. Then I tried again. I wrenched the knife out and attempted another forceful blow on the banana trunk. The second attempt entered it about ten centimeters away from the first attempt. I took another breather and thought that I was indeed a stupid fool. I could not even strike the same spot and had wasted my energy. I decided to use a different technique on my third attempt. This time, I regulated my breathing to ensure that I was first taking deep, long breaths. Then I made multiple small stabs at one spot. In a moment, the banana plant fell over. I lay down again and rested until I had recovered some energy. When I felt strong enough, I cut the banana plant with one swift slice. I peeled off its sheath and sucked the unripe meat inside. It tasted bitter and astringent. Moreover, it was sticky so I could not drink it like water. I slept there until the next morning.

Alien Antagonism

It was 21 April 1978 – the sixteenth day of my escape from Democratic Kampuchea. It had been one week since the Khmer New Year (Year of the Horse) had passed. I had stayed on Thai soil for one night. Circumstances had forced me to flee to this foreign land to avoid execution by the barbaric Khmer Rouge. My only thought was of my immediate future. Would the Thais have compassion or mercy on me and let me live among them or not? How would they treat me?

I resolved to be brave and take in my stride whatever was to come. My life dangling from the cliff of death was over. Puk Kim and Hian Lai had been my fellow companions on this journey. I highly respected and trusted them. They were physically stronger than me, yet they had died nine days ago. I was in agony from both physical and psychological pains.

Both my legs were injured and infected. Shooting pains raked me, sapping all my energy. In addition, hunger and thirst ravaged my body beyond my endurance. I tried to quench my thirst by sucking on a banana shoot, but this desiccated my throat even more. I pushed ahead on my buttocks across the burning old plantation and came to another which was being raked. A man and a child were pulling a plow back and forth, tilling the soil.

I scuttled directly towards the man, still on my backside. Around fifty meters from him, I shouted "Brother! Brother!" in the Thai language and waved my hands at him. He was startled and recoiled, dragging the plow and boy away. I shouted even louder a second time and then, a third time before he put down the plow and came towards me.

I still remember that they held me by my armpits, one on each side, and towed me facing up across the field. I fainted after this.

I did not know how long I had passed out. Suddenly, I heard Thai being spoken by people hovering above me. I opened my eyes to see many faces and pairs of eyes staring at me. I did not know where I was. My mouth was as dry as paper. Suddenly the cool sensation of water on a metal spoon touched my lips. I knew instantly that these kind people were giving me water. Water was my lifeline. I struggled to wrest the metal bowl of water from the hand of that generous and charitable person feeding me because I was too thirsty to drink by the spoon. My uncouth gesture was unsuccessful. Later, after this person had left, I managed to grab it from another person and gulped down the water until the bowl was empty. I lifted my hands to express my gratitude to all these kind strangers and to seek forgiveness for my boorishness.

I sat up by myself and observed that I was near a big road with fast-moving traffic. Passersby gawked and smirked at my cadaver-like body. I was just another one of those dirty and detestable Khmers.

When I had a little more energy, they put me on a motorcycle ("moto" in Khmer) and transported me to a mountain with a military fortress on top. They put me down from the moto under the shade of a tree and then left.

An instant later, two soldiers came directly towards me. One questioned me while the other interpreted.

The initial questioning went like this:

"Hungry or not?"

I responded, "I'm very hungry."

"Where did you come from?"

I replied, "I came from Khmer territory."

"Why did you flee?"

"They wanted to kill me."

"Why? Because you are a lazy bum?"

"It's not like this."

"Because you betrayed them?"

"I'm a new citizen they wanted to kill."

"What is a new citizen?"

"A new citizen is someone who lived outside the revolutionary regime before 17 April 1975."

"What did you do there?"

"I worked in the plantation."

"Take out everything you have now!"

I put my things on the ground, including my scarf with the religious inscription now faded to a pale color after my repeated sucking; one hundred pieces of mistletoes; some vines for tying things; a belt and the compass.

"Take this down from your neck!"

"Yes, sir but it contains only the ashes of my late father."

"Pull it down and let me see!"

"Yes, sir but it's purely my father's ashes. I cannot pull it down, sir. Please understand and help."

That soldier's hand crushed down on the small sachet that my wife had sewed to keep my late father's ashes, which was suspended from my neck by a cotton thread. (She had made two other such small sachets to keep the remaining ashes for my two eldest sons, so that the relics could be retained until the day we could return to our village.)

After that, they propped me up and searched me. Lastly, they tucked their hands into my pockets and found the sapphire ring that my friend, Tang Srang had given to me in 1973. (I only had a shirt and a pair of shorts on me. I had left the forest naked like this because my long pants were too heavy.) They took the sapphire ring and sat me down again.

They then brought and placed a large bowl of porridge with a spoon in front of me. The delicious aroma of the porridge made me forget my suffering, regret and indignity, even as I bemoaned the robbery of my sapphire ring. I quickly gobbled up the watery porridge. It tasted like divine food to me and I cleaned up the whole bowl.

One of the soldiers was not satisfied and returned. He ordered me to untie the bandages on both my legs. I did as I was told. When the bandages fell off, I saw a few maggots squirming out from my wounds. He ordered me to re-bandage them. I asked for permission to discard the old bandages and tore my remaining *krama* into new strips to wrap my wounds. My legs were still throbbing and hurting but a little hope returned to my heart.

Suddenly, a big four-tonner used for ferrying soldiers came roaring up and stopped in front of me. Five soldiers were on it, together with various equipment and weapons on a long bench. My interrogator ordered them to lift me onto the truck. Then a soldier on board blindfolded me with a piece of black cloth. All my hope vaporized. I shouted in English, "Please sirs, take me to the International Red Cross refuge." I heard a sound replying, "Agreed."

I rode in that truck for over an hour. When it stopped, a hand pulled me down onto the ground. I felt sick from kinetosis (motion sickness). They tore off my blindfold. Then the truck departed through a guarded gate, which slammed shut after it.

I sat on the ground while my eyes accustomed themselves to the view around me. I saw a white building with two floors at its back. There was a big *Snuol* (rosewood) tree on one side and a garden directly in front of the building. A row of floodlights lined the back of the building along one of its sides. Below the *Snuol* tree was a large, flat, open space with a pile of dead old trees. The place was protected by a high cement wall with barbed wire on top. It was quiet and deserted. I thought that perhaps this was the office of the Red Cross or the residence of an important man.

One moment later, I saw a half-naked old man wearing only shorts emerging from the building towards me. He walked past me to look at something near the wall but completely ignored my presence. I thought that as a newcomer, I should greet him. When he was returning to the building, I called out to him, "Salutations, *Loak Our!*"

(*"Loak Our"* is a customary form of address, conveying utmost respect, used in the northwestern region of Cambodia.)

"Please, Master *Loak Our*, save me. I am happy to shelter under the shadow of *Loak Our.*"

He yelled back at me, "Who shelter under whose shadow?!! You have no eyes or have eyes but cannot see the high barrier wall blocking even the clouds here?!! This is a prison, but you don't know, do you? There is no chance of getting out, ever!"

I was distraught. I had no hope after hearing the words of that old man. I sat there rigidly and alone until evening when some guards escorted about ten prisoners into the compound. Each prisoner had iron shackles on his ankles and chains on his forearms. The prisoners had to lift their arms to avoid the metal chains touching the ground. All of them were happy to see me, unlike the old man I had met earlier. We chatted and asked about each other like brothers.

One of them named Men took care of me more than the others. (Until today, I miss him tremendously, because he was a true friend who performed numerous good deeds to help me.) A guard ordered me to bathe in the pond but I replied that I could not do so without help as both my legs were injured. Men supported me to the edge of the pond. The guard prevented Men from helping me any further by shouting in Thai, "It (a derogatory term when used to refer to a human) can journey from Kampuchea to Thailand but cannot walk to bathe inside the pond. Do not help it!"

After the guard left, Men took a pail to scoop water from the pond and sprinkled it over me. I scrubbed my body and clothes clean and drank water until I was full. We did not have soap but I washed my wounds and re-bandaged them with my remaining *krama*.

My injuries were causing me great misery. My left leg from the sole to the ankle was deep red, inflamed and bulging. The right leg from the ankle to the knee was similarly engorged and angry. Both legs were infected and bloated to bursting point. They periodically emitted throbbing pains.

That evening, they rationed our food. Each prisoner received a bowl of rice, some soup and a few fried beans. I received the food with gratitude and relished the delicious taste of this simple meal that I had not tasted since the Khmer Rouge had taken control of the country. That night, I was given my own bed on the lower deck. I slept through the night.

The next morning, Men descended from the upper deck to wake me up. He supported me as I walked to wash my face. My legs were still swollen and I struggled with the pain. I started to have spasms whenever I turned my body. I dreaded when flies came hovering above my wounds because my miserable body would twist and jerk suddenly. The paroxysm would end as unpredictably as it had started. My convulsions started only at this detention center.

That morning, the chief of the detention center came with some guards to question me about my escape. I could not answer them coherently because we were constantly interrupted by my seizures. I begged the chief for mercy to give me some medicines to treat my condition. He told me to write down the prescription so that he could buy them from a pharmacy. I took the opportunity to ask him to inform Towkay Kheang, the proprietor of a large pharmacy in Aranya, that I was here and needed his help. About two hours later, the chief returned with a strip of painkiller and said that the anti-convulsion medicines I prescribed were unavailable. Moreover, he said that Towkay Kheang denied knowing anyone with my name.

I was thankful for the painkiller. It allowed me to answer the chief's questioning, which lasted about one hour.

The next day, he returned to ask some more questions. I had to be excused again because pain was raking me and I could not answer him. The painkiller was effective for only a short while. I wondered if I had caught tetanus, even though I had received all kinds of anti-tetanus injections when I was a student.

That evening, a new group of refugees arrived. There were a few casualties among them. They had been shot by the Khmer Rouge on their arms or legs but were not seriously wounded. None had received treatment. The most critical case was a man who was shot straight through his neck. The bullet had punctured his neck from the front to the back but he survived. Except for him, the rest were shackled individually and chained together.

When night fell, I had to share my bed with another person. Even though I was in great pain myself, I was very worried about the condition of the man with the neck injury. I examined his body with my hand and found him cold to touch. I gave him a large pair of pants and used a mosquito net for myself. Men helped to cover him with the pants, which reached to his neck.

The next morning, the guards assembled us to pay respect to the Thai national anthem and their king. Then they issued us our work orders.

That man with the neck injury and I did not receive any work. We sat on the pile of dead trees beneath the *Snuol* tree, waiting for lunch time. We were famished and displayed the same symptoms as all the others. Our stomachs churned ferociously at the sounds of a spoon striking a plate (signifying meal times) that echoed from the military fortress behind this detention center. This detention center was under the control of the military police (also known as the provost).

I observed that there were three officers who came to work regularly every day and night. One was named Yong and had the rank of *Moo*, roughly equivalent to a master sergeant in the Khmer army. He alternated his shift with another *Moo* whose name I did not know. There was another officer above them with the rank of *Ja*, approximately equivalent to a sergeant major in the Khmer army (or first sergeant in the US army). They had many other guards assisting them. They appointed one Khmer who was most adept at currying favors and proficient in the Thai language to watch over all of us.

That man was named Grandfather Sa Rearng. He and he alone had absolute power over all of us. He could scold, insult, reproach or wallop any one of us with impunity. We were all scared of him because he was the translator for the guards. He could twist our words to instigate trouble for us as he wished. This was the man I had addressed as *Loak Our* on my day of arrival.

There was another old man called Grandfather Om who received more responsibility than the rest of us. I had seen him in the compound before the others when I first arrived. He was the silent type but gruff in speech when scolding us.

Another person appointed by the guards to control us was the son of a Khmer Chinese who ladled out our food every day. Whoever made him happy would receive more food as he dished out our rice soup separately. On the other hand, anyone who crossed him would be punished by receiving a smaller ration or be hit on the head with the ladle by him for lacking good manners.

At this detention center, we were all refugees with no safeguards on our lives or health. We felt that the guards and other soldiers who entered this compound treated us with contempt and enmity. They stared at us with hostility as if we were hardcore criminals or primitive life forms. They could order us to do whatever they wished and often threatened to execute us. We trembled at their sight. I heard from the others' weeping and sobbing about this vicious group. If we made even a small mistake, such as not cleaning our feet before entering a room or not showing respect to the Thai monarchy, they would lug us to the nearby prison cell where we could even be beaten to death. They could torture us by beating, kicking or stomping on us as they liked.

Every morning and afternoon, they shackled those of us with energy to work inside the fortress. At meal times, they gave us each a bowl of rice with water poured on it. Gradually, all of us lost weight until there was only skin covering our bones. We hardly defecated because there was no residue waste inside our bodies. Even before the shoots of the shrubs that they planted around the pond to make a protective barrier had grown, many of us were dead. Famine and exhaustion, coupled with the endless insults, mockery and threats on the Khmers from the Thai guards sickened me until I wished to die. If I had known that the Thai guards were so mean, I would happily let the Khmer Rouge execute me at the mouth of the village. At least the Khmer Rouge had Khmer blood too. Even under the Khmer Rouge, where we were starving and had to labor very hard, it was not as bad as this. I was absolutely disheartened.

There was only one woman in our group. She was a modest person of average build, hardworking and friendly with everyone. All of us slept in a big room but we installed a screen to give her some space to herself. Every night, when the "*Moo*-without-a-name" (below *Moo* Yong) was on duty, he would come and drag her out. She would not return until the next morning. We were all deeply pained and aggrieved by her ordeal as we were all Khmer refugees helpless against the violent rape by that *Moo*. We could only sympathize with her silently.

As for *Moo* Yong, he was a mature and understanding person who was willing to help us.

My injuries started to cause me great suffering. Both of my lower legs were swollen stiff and ached intolerably. I clasped my legs in an attempt to control the pain but cried out aloud irrepressibly after some time. I shouted non-stop all day and all night. The excruciating pain made me want to give up. I shouted to the King of Death to let me die quickly.

Two days after my pain had subsided somewhat, a guard ordered Saran (who had been shot in the neck) to take the garbage cart and dump me at the mortuary of the military hospital. Saran lifted me onto the cart and pushed me from the detention center to the hospital. A short distance from the detention center, we ran into a group of new recruits. A few of them walked towards us and ordered me to descend from the cart. They wanted Saran to get on it and for me to push him back to where we came from. We did not understand the Thai language but understood from their gestures what they wanted us to do. Saran and I saluted them and gesticulated that I was seriously injured and could not descend from the cart but they continued yelling for us to comply with their instruction. Luckily, a whistle blew repeatedly just then. This was a signal for them to assemble for a meeting. They stopped bothering us and left.

Saran pushed the cart with me on it farther on. We reached the hospital yard and coincidentally, a young doctor with a stethoscope hanging from his neck walked by. Even though my legs were causing me much grief, my mind was still crystal clear. I called out to him in English and Thai to help me, telling him that I had been a doctor too in Cambodia. He nodded his head and signaled for Saran to push me to a building on the left.

A short while later, that doctor entered the building and told Saran to push the garbage cart to a corner. A nurse lifted me onto the treatment bed. The doctor tested me by asking, "Since you are a doctor, which medicines should be used to treat your condition?" He pointed to the medicine cabinet along one of the walls. I did as asked and he nodded in agreement.

According to his instructions, the nurse injected me with the medicines and washed my wounds gingerly. They injected me with the medicines in quantities far beyond the normal dosage. For example, the medicine to treat tetanus called Tetanol was usually administered in only one to two vials. However, I saw them injecting me with eleven ampoules at one shot. As for penicillin, they injected me with two million units together with one pill of the antibiotic streptomycin. I dared not challenge the excessive dosage they were giving me because I thought it was better to die from an overdose than to endure this intolerable pain. After they had treated me, they attended to Saran.

It was Saran's good luck that the bullet, which went straight through his neck from the front to the back, did not puncture any vital points on his body. This was good fortune within a great misfortune.

After receiving treatment, my pain diminished considerably. I thanked the kind doctor and nurse for saving my life. Saran pushed me on the garbage cart back to the detention center.

The two of us shared many memories together. From that day onwards, my condition progressively improved. One month later, I could stand and even walk a little. Saran's injury also healed.

Not getting enough food meant that we recovered very slowly. We received only enough food to keep us alive or to perish slowly one by one.

One night, I was worried about a swelling near my anus. It was firm but painless. I examined it with my hand and suddenly, it dropped off in a small lump. I took it to inspect under the light and was completely horrified to find a parasitic leech. I had seen such bloodsuckers drinking the blood from water buffaloes or dogs before. Now one was sucking my blood until its body became round like a small ball.

Around that time, a new refugee named Or gave me twenty baht. This money for me at that time had immeasurable value. I used it to buy cigarettes, sugar and medicines to treat my illness.

About two months passed. One night, I dreamt of my father. He told me to endure a little longer. He wanted me to wait for him to take me to a wat (temple) where I would meet some companions. After I had eaten my fill, he took me out of the wat. Then he took a small hut that looked like a small ancestral shrine at the mouth of a creek and threw it into the water. He instructed me to jump on that hut to cross to the other side.

I woke up from this dream full of hope because it was an extraordinary dream. Would my deceased father (who died when we were evacuated to Toul Kork village in September 1975) really come to help me? It made me optimistic anyway.

Two days later, the guards came to recruit volunteers to fight against the Khmer Rouge at the border. All of us – young or old, healthy or sick – volunteered together. However, they picked only those who were strong and healthy. The next day, they announced the names of the chosen ones who boarded a truck in front of the fortress. Both my good friends, Men and Saran left me that day. They had gone before me to fight the Khmer Rouge inside our country. Would we ever meet again? I felt abandoned and wondered when I could leave and join them.

Neither of my legs had recovered fully. They were still painful, bruised and numb. I still did not have the strength to walk long distances. Strangely, I no longer experienced the gastritis that had plagued me since my youth. I had endured it for as long as I could remember and it could not be cured. I had to take medicines every day to control it or I would suffer badly. During the Khmer Rouge regime when modern medicines were unavailable, I treated it using traditional remedies, one of which had come to me in a dream. That remedy was as potent as modern drugs to alleviate my condition. Suddenly, I was completely cured of this malady, which left me pondering how this had come about.

One morning two weeks later, the guards assembled us and after a roll call, informed us that we would be sent for sentencing at a courthouse in Kabin district. We were to reply to the judge that we had only arrived the night before. Anyone who responded differently would face the consequences upon our return. We boarded the truck waiting for us. Along the way, we were excited to see the scenery of the countryside and other interesting views that we had not seen for a long time.

We arrived at the courthouse about one hour later. Two guards escorted us inside where they let us sit on chairs on a porch facing a big courthouse. We were captivated by the endless stream of people coming in and going out. They too stared at us, some with puzzled looks and others with pity as they observed our skeletal bodies wearing torn rags as clothes.

I was lost in time looking at them when a guard came for us. We were led into the court and sat on the chairs silently and solemnly. A court clerk called out our names one by one and we had to stand up when called. After that, a judge with a Chinese appearance wearing a long black robe hurriedly entered. He stood at the center of a long table and announced that (based on what I remember according to the Khmer translation) all of us had entered Thailand illegally. Accordingly to Thai laws, we were sentenced to jail for eighteen hours and a fine of forty baht. If we could not pay, our jail time would be increased in lieu of the fine. The session was then adjourned and the judge left.

The guards escorted us out from the courthouse to a detention center in Kabin. Along the way, we walked in neat rows with one guard in front and another at the back. We walked silently under their watchful eyes, absorbed by the views that greeted us. There was a bustling market with many shops selling all kinds of merchandise. The houses were not very tall and were similar to what we had in Cambodia before the war. The difference was that there were many more things to buy here.

We were trooping along when a monk descended from a *remorque* and stood by our side. The Venerable threw coins straight at us. I caught one, though I did not know its value. I wanted to exchange it for some food. Along the pavement were sellers hawking packets of iced coffee hanging from their carts. Overwhelmed by hunger and thirst, I unthinkingly left my place in the line and took a packet of iced coffee from one of the carts. I placed the coin from the monk on the cart to pay for it and took a sip of the iced coffee. Suddenly, my packet of iced coffee was snatched from my hand. From one hand to another, only sipping sounds were heard until the drink was completely finished. We knew again the taste of iced coffee, which we had not savored for three years.

I was drowning in the delicious aroma and taste of that iced coffee when a hand grabbed my shoulder. I quickly turned my head and saw that it was the iced coffee seller. She gestured to say that I still owed her money. I was flabbergasted – I had no more money. Thankfully, a guard came to my rescue. He sent her away by telling her that I was entitled to a discount because we were all aliens without money and that the one baht I had paid was given by the monk just now. At that time, I felt no embarrassment because my misery was far greater than any shame. We were people of no value – just humans waiting to die, either through starvation or execution. I often heard rumors that they intended to barter us to the Khmer Rouge for rice.

When we reached the Kabin detention center, they shoved us into a metal cage measuring four meters by four meters with a height of about two and a half meters. The cage had very strong metal bars and support columns. It was located in a gully about forty centimeters underground. In the middle of the cage was a metal pail serving as our toilet. There were around twenty criminals inside. We did not have enough space to stretch our legs. We curled our bodies, facing each other, with our backs against the metal bars. The whole place was crowded, oppressive and suffocating.

We were locked up in this cage in the afternoon. When evening arrived, we were each given a bowl of rice soup.

We were famished after being cramped into this small space for many hours without any food or drink. That afternoon, I chanced upon a plate of rice for the cat. The sight of it made me ravenous. I poked my leg through the gaps between the metal bars in an attempt to pinch that plate of rice, but it was too far away. I was absolutely thwarted and envious that the lucky cat should have so much food to eat that it did not bother finishing the rice. I was convinced that if they kept us like this for two days, some of us would die.

The next morning, they forced us out from the cage to clean ourselves and to empty the waste in that metal pail. We stretched our cramped bodies a bit before they ordered us back into the cage. They detained us in this manner for another day. In the evening, they transported us back to the *Snuol* Tree Detention Center. We were relieved to be back as it was better than being in the cage. That night, they gave us more rice than usual.

Maya: Make-Believe

All the world's a stage,
And all the men and women merely players.
They have their exits and their entrances...

Shakespeare, ***As You Like It***

Two days later, they ordered all of us remaining at the detention center to board a truck at Aranya town at dawn. Each of us received a pack of rice and a packet of water. All of us were worried and apprehensive as we did not know the purpose of this journey. Where were they taking us? This question was on all of our minds. We spent our time on the truck repeatedly dozing off and jolting awake. In the afternoon, we reached a place none of us knew.

The truck came to a silent stop and its engine stilled. We were prohibited from leaving it. If we needed to pee, we had to ask permission from the guards, who would accompany us. Some kind villagers there gave us drinking water and packs of rice. Later, the truck drove on a little farther until it was past midnight. It stopped before a temple.

It had been raining for more than two hours with no sign of it stopping soon. We slept quietly on board the truck. When it stopped in front of a wat, I remembered my dream from a few nights ago. In it, my late father had told me to be patient. He first took me to a temple before taking me out again to cross a creek. Now I had indeed arrived before a temple with bright flashing lightbulbs on my left. Was this the temple from my dream?

When the rain abated to a drizzle, the building on my right that had been dark and silent suddenly lit up and bathed the gateway in light. We could see many rows of low buildings behind. Many guards stood at attention right in front of the gateway where the truck was parked. One guard called out our names individually from a register and we had to descend from the truck when called to enter the building on the right.

We filed into that building, which served as the guards' office. At the back of this office was a wide open yard. Along its four sides were long buildings detached from each other. There was another small house near the guards' office that was used as a store.

The guards ordered us to dry ourselves in the middle of the yard as we were drenched from the rain. After counting the number of people, they let us rest there until the next morning. We were all soaking wet and exhausted. We looked for a dry slope without water flowing on it so that we could lie down and sleep. I slept well, until nearly daybreak. I woke up startled when I caught sight of a shadowy figure near my feet. I opened my eyes wide and clearly saw a man kneeling there. I asked him, "Brother, why are you kneeling here?"

He replied, "I came to invite Brother to come with me."

I asked him how he knew me. He replied that he had seen in a dream that I must go with him.

I was flummoxed by that man's response. Was my life dictated by dreams? What was this connection between my life and dreams? Sometimes, they were my own dreams but sometimes, other people's dreams. I did not believe in dreams before but now, they were influencing and informing me whenever I felt lost. I got up from my slumber and went with him to the building where he stayed.

Inside it, he had cleared a spacious room for himself and his son who was asleep. He gave me a pillow and prepared a sleeping place for me. I had a mosquito net that I had always used since I arrived at the *Snuol* Tree Detention Center at Aranya. At that time, I was very sick, with alternating fever and chill. One of my friends took this old mosquito net from a corner of the wall to cover me. The man took my mosquito net to shake off its dust. I saw his good heart, which made me trust him.

In the morning, all the buildings inside this detention center opened their doors to let the detainees out to use the toilets outside. A group of four to five youngsters headed straight towards me. All of them paid their respects to me. One of them introduced me to all his companions. They were respectful and addressed me as "Puk" (meaning "Father." The Khmer Rouge had instituted the practice for Cambodians to address all elders roughly the same age as their parents as "Puk" or "Mak" meaning "Mother"). I was taken aback as I did not know them. One of them saw my quizzical expression and explained, "Puk, I was a member of the Snuol Kaong mobile unit. Puk gave me my eye medication every time my father left to work far away." I apologized that I could not remember them because the mobile unit had so many members.

One of them whispered to me that the man I stayed with the night before was named Roeung. His son was named Ley. He said Roeung had a tendency to overdo things, like a fire that burned everything in its path. All the detainees disliked him. They invited me to stay with them at their building and offered to serve me as their father.

I hesitated to accept their sincere invitation. Roeung had kneeled by my side and respectfully invited me to stay with him the night before and I had received his attentive assistance. I replied to them that I would stay with Roeung for the time being. If I were to be uncomfortable here, I would go and stay with them. All of them agreed with my decision.

Roeung came back from washing my mosquito net and called me to take a bath. He escorted me to the reservoir. He swept the dust off my body and bathed me with care. I realized that his character was not like I had been told. We returned from the reservoir together. He took a *krama* to dry me and brought a shirt for me like I was his patron. When we were done, I sat down on a mat to chat with him. Without any warning, he kneeled down and bowed to me three times, saying, "From this time onwards, I ask Brother to treat me like your own younger brother." I readily agreed, because we were sworn brothers united in our misery. I stayed happily with Roeung and his son, Ley. The group of youth continued to treat me like their father.

This refugee camp we called Borei Ram (in Thai: Buriram) was formerly a prison under the Buriram provincial administration. In view of the increasing number of Khmer refugees, the provincial government decided to isolate the Thai criminals in a new prison. Hence, this place was also called "the old prison."

Our lives were still regimented inside this camp as the previous prison wardens continued to run it, except that we were not shackled or chained anymore. We were given food twice a day for lunch and dinner. There was only one menu: water, a small plate of extremely diluted *prahok* (fermented fish sauce), six pieces of fried eggplant and one pathetic scoop of rice. The rice was not enough to fill our stomachs. The youth who adopted me as their father each gave me some of their rice so that I would have enough to eat. Thanks to them, I slowly regained some meat and blood.

One day, a vein spontaneously burst from one of my leg wounds. I teased it out and squeezed out all the pus. This vein was almost twenty centimeters long. It had detached from the same spot the military doctor at Aranya cleaned when I was still at the *Snuol* Tree Detention Center. This ruptured vein was the reason why the lesion in front would not seal. Once I excised it, my ulcer healed.

Time passed by slowly at first. The other refugees and I always gathered to chat. We missed our country and our families. We wanted to fight and liberate our country from the grip of the savage group ruling Democratic Kampuchea. Before 1970, when Samdech Preah Norodom Sihanouk was the Royal Chief of State, he named them Khmer Rouge because they had communist inclination ("rouge" is the French word for "red" and "Khmer Rouge" means the "Red Khmers").

The number of refugees in the camp mushroomed to five hundred. We always sought information on the latest situation from the newcomers. We knew about the strangulating oppression of the Khmer Rouge that continued killing the people. On top of that, they were now killing each other within the Organization. One group of Khmer Rouge from the southwest region had swooped down to sweep clean the groups in the other regions. The older generations of Khmer Rouge leaders were taken away for re-education. The number of people fleeing the cooperatives kept increasing but this caused the Khmer Rouge to tighten its grip even more. Its army hunted down the escapees like prey. There were many more people waiting in fear than those who tried to escape. Even fewer made it across the border to become refugees. The Khmer Rouge waited at the border where they shot dead any Thai soldier or Khmer escapee they saw. Some groups fled with more than one hundred members but in the end, only about ten or so arrived alive at the refugee camp.

I wondered how many more people the Khmer Rouge had killed that we had no news about. Oh, Khmers! We had risked our lives to cross the border in order to be "free," all because of a power struggle between Khmers and Khmers. The Khmer state had lost nearly all its territory because of this war. When would it stop?

Instead, we became unwelcomed refugees who had fled far from our villages, far from our families, to seek help from a foreign government, only to realize too late that we should have known to love our own country.

We organized ourselves to return to fight and give freedom back to the Khmer people. We covertly formed ourselves into sections, squads and platoons, with sixteen young captains and a defined chain of command. Our plan was to prepare in advance, pending the time when we could get the Thai government's support to leave the refugee camp and return to fight the Khmer Rouge. Each of us was impatient for the day to come.

One day, the International Red Cross received permission to visit this refugee camp. I immediately contacted the American CIA through my friend, a Canadian doctor. Shortly after, I received a visit from an influential CIA agent who had crossed the border from Poipet into Thailand. I described to him my perceptions of the current situation in Cambodia and requested support from the United States of America. He replied that it was easy to theorize from an armchair. He said that Puk Lon Nol had carted armor and planes from the United States to fight the Khmer Rouge yet he did not win. Now, we asked for only five hundred guns and expected to overthrow the Khmer Rouge with these. I tried hard to explain to him that the tide had turned. During Lon Nol's time, the people supported the Khmer Rouge, but now they hated it. They were just biding their time for an opportunity to strike back. He told me that he would convey my request for his headquarters' consideration. I added that if five hundred guns were not possible, we would accept two hundred. I never heard from him again.

(I only found out later, when I had gone to live in France, that the Americans and Thais supported and supplied weapons to the Khmer Rouge to fight against the Vietnamese, who were fronting the Khmer Blanc – the White Khmers – the group defeated by the Khmer Rouge.)

Not long after, the refugee camp administration discovered our increasing fervor to topple the Khmer Rouge. To defuse the tension, it forbade the guards from threatening to deport us back to fight with the Khmer Rouge. Moreover, they ordered one man named Sao Say Near to report to the guards' office. After that, they called me to meet him there.

Sao Say Near was of average build, had clear skin and was about forty years old. He was a fetching man with charming manners. He spoke modestly and pleasantly. When queried, he replied that he was from Phnom Penh. I saw many scars and wounds on his head and legs. When we met, I immediately sensed that he was a patriot. He spoke to me like an older brother would to a younger brother with compassion and homesickness in his voice. I had sympathy for him too. I understood from the unspoken meaning underlying his speech that he could not speak freely because he was scared of the Thai guards. He said to me that, "We are still prisoners along the border. We lack almost everything. Let's wait and see first." He then gave me fifty baht and we parted ways.

I felt bad for him but I also recognized immediately that he was a spy in the talons of the Thais. Oh, Khmers! We need to love our own country! We escaped from the claws of the Khmer Rouge only to fall into the clutches of an alien country. Was this our destiny? They used us as they deemed fit until the day we died. We were simply pawns to be manipulated in their game.

I fell ill. I was homesick and missed my wife and family greatly. I was sick from morning till night, whatever I was doing. This was the disease of displaced people who were left helpless and hopeless. The atmosphere within the refugee camp became even worse.

In the Khmer calendar, the fifteenth day during the waning moon of the tenth lunar month is Pchum Ben day.

Pchum Ben is a major traditional festival celebrated by the Khmer Buddhists. From the first to the fourteenth day of the waning moon in the tenth lunar month, there is a ceremony called "to carry or to offer the rice balls." The fifteenth day itself is Pchum Ben day. The festival is organized to consecrate offerings of food and drinks and to dedicate merits to our ancestors. Three days of public holidays are allotted each year for this festival, from the fourteenth to the sixteenth day, during the waning moon in the tenth lunar month.

All of us in the refugee camp knew about this important festival because we could see the phases of the moon. However, we had lost track of time since the Khmer Rouge came into power. It had been a long time since we last honored our traditions. Suddenly, we heard from some Thai people that some five ethnic Khmers had come to distribute many of the banana rice cakes and sweet coconut rice cakes that were traditionally prepared for the Pchum Ben. We received confirmation from the leader of this group that Pchum Ben had just passed.

Our esteemed visitors had deep sympathy for our plight. They organized a traditional bamboo dance for us, but this increased our homesickness. They stayed to chat with us for a long time until the guards told them to leave. The point of their visit was to take some of us out from the refugee camp to live with them in the village. Moreover, some of them had young, lovely daughters of marriageable age whom they wish to wed to ethnic Khmers. They would divide their wealth, including paddy fields, many hectares of land and their cattle, with their future sons-in-law. The major caveat was that permission would first need to be obtained from the Thai Interior Ministry.

About one week later, they returned with tears in their eyes. They related dismally that the chief at the ministry had responded to their request by saying, "Wouldn't it be better to give your daughter to a dog than to a Khmer?" These were the insulting words from the Thai authorities supervising us (if they were truly what the official uttered).

When two nations have fallen out, each would treat the other's citizens with derision and contempt as being inferior. What had we done to deserve such disrespect? We are Khmer citizens who live upright, moral lives. Our only crime was that we had to flee our own country to become aliens in another.

When our country faces calamity or unrest, we will suffer with it. When our country experiences peace and progress, we will also prosper with it. Therefore, please do not take politics as a joke, because, in the words of Mr. In Tam (a Khmer Republican), "A bullet fired from a gun can kill one person but words expressed from the mouth of a politician can kill hundreds."

One morning, a group of us asked for permission to go out for a look at the market. I tagged along. I was walking and taking in the sights of this big market when I spotted a handicapped, frumpy, middle-aged woman selling dried tobacco leaves from a small round basket. She had sold most of it and there was only some left. I asked her how much it would cost, but she told me to unfurl the hem of my *krama* instead. I protested that all I wanted was to buy one stick of tobacco to smoke but she was insistent. I unfurled the hem of my *krama* a little. The next thing I knew, she was pouring her remaining tobacco into that opening. I carefully unrolled the rest of my *krama* hem to prevent any spillage. She wrapped my *krama* that now held all her remaining tobacco and handed it back to me, saying, "Take it and go! We are all Khmers. When one group of Khmers suffers, we highland Khmers must also help."

I thanked her with tears in my eyes. Just a while before, I had thought that she looked like a very poor rural villager. Yet, she gave me all her remaining tobacco. Having given me all that she had, how would she go back home? Moreover, her crippled body made me tremble at my own ugliness and superficiality. Beyond her unflattering appearance, she had a heart full of goodness, generosity and patriotism. How many Khmers love their country and people straightforwardly like this honest highlander?

I pay my highest respects to her. All Khmers, whether from the highlands, the midlands or the lowlands, should emulate her love for our country and fellowmen.

One day, the Thai authorities transported some musical instruments for safekeeping inside the store. There were some legal issues surrounding them. We were prisoners with much spare time on our hands and were always bored. When we saw so many different musical instruments that we had not seen for a long time before us, we crowded around to ogle at them. One of the guards on duty came out and asked if we knew all these instruments. One man replied affirmatively. He asked again if we knew how to play them. Again, that man said yes.

"So, you want to play or not?"

That guard allowed those who knew how to play the musical instruments to try. They played a few stanzas before the guard stopped them. He had to get permission from above first.

A few days later, the second deputy provincial governor visited the refugee camp. He was responsible for the provincial jail and this refugee camp we were staying in. Someone told me that he was an ethnic Khmer in Buriram. I was very pleased to hear this as I thought that if this was true, he would surely help to alleviate our suffering.

I hurried to pay my respect to him and thanked him for taking the time to meet us. He spoke Khmer fluently. He asked about our situation and we informed him about our hardships and low morale because we missed our country and families. Moreover, we highlighted to him that none of us would run away from the camp (since we had nowhere else to go) and asked him to reduce the restrictions on us. Some inmates had suffered to death from feelings of homesickness, boredom, worry and depression because the authorities did not allow us to go out at all.

After listening to us, he granted us the right to ask for permission to go out; to meet together to exercise or play sports within the camp compound; and to practice music in the evenings. He said that he would come and test our musical aptitude one day. We were deeply thankful for his understanding and compassion.

The eagerly-anticipated day to assess the Khmer refugees' musical talents arrived. Under the patronage of the deputy provincial governor of Buriram province, many officials, chiefs, guards and villagers attended the concert. They were seated in the VIP rows.

We felt pride welling up within us to be able to perform for such distinguished guests. We elected a leader and also competed among ourselves.

The concert took place in the canteen. We had rearranged the dining tables to form a stage. Our honored guests sat in the front rows while the examiners sat on chairs arranged in a row on one side of the stage. The non-performing refugees sat at the back.

The music announcing the start of the program was played. Examiners called the candidates to sing one by one. They all sang sentimental and sorrowful Khmer songs that were heart breaking. Many candidates sang till the end even though some of them had to pause when they became too emotional. There was one singer who choked in the middle of a song but continued singing till the end. Some of them sobbed while singing.

One candidate named Khlern bawled out his piece from the beginning. He sang melodiously until he came to the line, "lift the mosquito net to see my child." He kneeled down on one knee and slowly raised his hand as if he was lifting a mosquito net. Then he hanged his head down low like he was gazing at his child sleeping on a mat. Abruptly, he fell flat on the stage.

All the examiners huddled together in fright. The music stopped. The candidate continued lying there motionless. The examiners got someone to go upstage to check on him. He suddenly sprang up, kicking and shouting that he wanted to kill himself. All the examiners quickly got up and had him carried offstage. This incident caused many members of the audience to weep uncontrollably.

The first night concert by the Khmer refugees ended in tears. The memory of this night was etched on the audience's minds. The next day, a group of people protested to the chief of the refugee camp. They wished to attend the next concert. The chief replied that the concert was simply for the refugees to overcome boredom and not meant for public viewing. The protestors were not satisfied and took their complaint to the provincial government. The deputy provincial governor agreed to let us perform again to appease this group of protestors.

This time, we deliberated together and decided that we would stage a play as well as perform the coconut shell dance. To stage a play requires many hours of rehearsal. The guards gave us ten days to rehearse. We practiced all day and all night. In our group, there were no trained actors or dancers so we had to stage a very simple story. I was responsible for writing the script. A few youth were in charge of the coconut shell dance.

One week later, the coconut shell dance by the Khmer youth took form. It was truly remarkable that the youth who knew nothing about the coconut shell dance could improvise and choreograph a new version, based on real life observations. They created a spectacular display matching any professional performance and received resounding acclaim. This is a testament to the Khmers' ingenious artistic gene.

As for my script, I had never studied or done any writing or editing, but in my college days I used to attend many Khmer New Year performances with my good friends. We only knew how to speak in our usual monotone, unlike the professionals' rhythmic stage utterances foretelling a character's disposition. Nonetheless, since we were now allowed to express ourselves, we attempted to show all the viewers that we took this work very seriously. We did not have any stage props or paraphernalia, except for the musical instruments loaned from the guards. We wore our old shabby clothes – they were the only ones we had anyway, apart from some clothes left behind by some ex-prisoners.

The day for our public performance came. We scrubbed ourselves clean even though we did not have any soap. We had put together a stage the night before using the dining tables and decorated it with the large leaves that we cut from outside the camp after getting the guards' permission.

Even before the appointed time, the crowds started to arrive. Our performance was free of charge. A large congregation of people amassed in front of the detention center. The chief had to increase the number of guards to cope with so many people. We were nervous, excited and happy all at the same time, to know that there were people interested in our show. We prayed silently for the souls of Khmer ancestors to channel into our bodies and give us strength and courage so that we would achieve success before this Thai audience with Khmer ancestry who understood the Khmer language.

We gobbled down our dinner hastily, which was watery *prahok* and fried eggplant like every day. We did not finish eating our rice because we saw the noisy crowds pouring in. The sight made us miss our families, siblings and country. Before the war, we too had gathered our loved ones to watch such performances in our own villages.

The show began. We did not have any curtains so the performers appeared from behind the stage. As soon as the music started, the all-male cast of dancers who were still in their prison attire started leaping and jumping most gloriously. Sounds of coconut shells tapping together were heard in tempo with the music. This spectacular act depicting a pair of male and female birds pecking, playing and chasing one another on the stage enraptured the viewers who dared not shut their eyes for fear of missing something. As soon as the dance stopped, thunderous applause reverberated throughout the canteen. All the actors stood shaking, impervious to the tears flowing down their cheeks. We took a fifteen-minute intermission.

The next act was a modern mime. All the actors kept silent and conveyed the story entirely through their body movements, gestures and facial expressions. The sharp, piercing sounds of the flute cut repeatedly through the completely silent canteen. A soft voice in the background narrated the glorious past of Cambodia. It was a country with abundance and prosperity. It was richly endowed with natural resources, from the small rivers, tributaries, and lakes to the seas full of fishes. Its soil was rich and fertile. The mountains, forests and trees provided all kinds of minerals and materials. It was an agricultural country modernizing towards industrialization. Its citizens did not lack anything and lived happily in harmony, solidarity and prosperity as the country progressed.

At this point, the sharp sounds of the flute were replaced by the low rumbling of the drum and trumpet. A metal tray was repeatedly struck to produce clashing sounds.

Now Kampuchea had become an ideological country. Its people were worn out by its enemy. The raging fire of war ignited and burned down the whole country until only ruins and destruction remained. To stay alive, the Khmers sought help from each other and fled to a neighboring country for shelter.

Sounds of the drum and tray stopped here, replaced by the flute and the violin.

When the music stopped, the performers – all men, but some dressed as women – walked onto the stage carrying various work tools such as digging hoes; the large flat baskets used for sifting rice; and spinning wheels for making cotton thread. They danced in step with the music, waiting for daybreak until they came to Cambodia at night. They walked long and searched hard for a big space where they could each sit down to work. They were glad to work hard in order to improve their lives.

Here, the narrative changed to say that the Khmers had now united to overthrow their enemy.

The soundscape reverted to the discordant clashing sounds.

The actors ran about onstage looking scared to depict them searching for a hiding place. Finally, the music changed to a forlorn piece played on the flute or violin. All the actors joined their hands and slowly descended from the stage in a row.

After this performance, one singer ascended onstage to express our sorrow and despair at being separated from our loved ones. The finale was by another solo singer who belted out a melodious sentimental song. Then, the orchestra played softly the music of *Sayonara* while all the performers went onstage and bowed to the audience.

The night performance ended on this subdued note, with camaraderie and silent gratification at our newly-achieved artistic success.

The next day, the guards allowed a few women from the provincial Department of Arts to interview the coconut shell dancers. They meticulously noted down the dance steps from one sequence to the other. They asked the dancers to demonstrate the dance again. We told them that the dance had been created from our imagination based on our memories so there was no precise choreography. They were very impressed to hear this.

One week later, the guards conveyed the news that a TV station in Bangkok belonging to the royal family wanted us to perform at a provincial festival. They would videotape our performance and broadcast it live to the whole country. We dared not be negligent with such a momentous task. We rehearsed again and again every day to prepare for it.

On the appointed day, a truck transported all our performers in the afternoon to the venue where we would be performing. We arrived at a very clean and spacious hall in our prisoner outfits. They allowed us to rehearse for a short while. Around seven in the evening, the official program started.

From behind the thick silk curtains, a popular male singer from Bangkok came onstage and started singing a sentimental song under the bright glare of the colorful stage lights. His voice was full but hoarse. The first stanza had just drifted away when the shrill, sharp voice of a little girl sliced through the air, giving us shudders. After this, it was our turn.

Our highly successful performance caused us to quiver. A member of the Thai royal family came to shake our hands and congratulate us. His Royal Highness expressed the wish for us to perform in Bangkok (according to the guards' translation). After our performance, two women of mixed Thai-Lao blood sang a happy song but they appeared affected by our act and sang loudly in a half-hearted way. We were sent back to the refugee camp before the end of the festival. We had the same food as usual that night, but we were satisfied.

The next day, they came to sell photos of our performance but each sheet cost five baht. Most of us had no money to buy the photos even though these mementos would have meant so much to us.

One week later, a group of provincial officials came and many of us went marching together with them to protest the barbaric deeds of the communist Khmer Rouge. (At that time, the Thai communists were spreading from the countryside and penetrating the bureaucracy, causing problems for the government.)

A little later, I heard that the Thai government had agreed to let the Chinese government transport weapons to the Khmer Rouge army through Thailand in exchange for the Chinese government's agreement to stop supporting the Thai communists. (The Khmer Rouge troops were fighting against the Vietnamese army at the Khmer-Vietnam border at that time.)

Perhaps as a result of this move, the Thai communists began to lose their influence from that time.

One morning, a military vehicle drove into the refugee camp, which was unusual. The officer on board the vehicle descended and ordered his men to find volunteers to go and build a fortress to defend against the Khmer Rouge. I went out to meet them and said that we would all volunteer together. We would go together as a group, not separately. If this could not be done, then none of us would go.

The chief replied that he could not take all of us at one go. He could only take four to ten persons each time. Immediately, soldiers on board the vehicle jumped down and abducted seven of our youth onto their vehicle, which promptly drove off.

We were incensed. We ran around frantically and consulted with each other extensively on how to protest against this violation of our rights by the Thai military. We wanted all seven youngsters back. These Thai soldiers were cowardly bullies who pounced on us unannounced and kidnapped our members.

From that day onwards, we stood ready to resist them at every opportunity. They would not be allowed to swoop on us from above easily again. I secretly wrote a letter in French to the French Embassy and the United Nations in Bangkok respectively. I sent the letters through a child to avoid arousing the guards' suspicions. This boy often ran errands for the guards so he was allowed free movement in and out from the refugee camp. I did not have money for postage and dared not ask for it from strangers, as I was afraid this would let the cat out of the bag.

The head of the provincial Department of Culture kept asking our group to perform on various occasions, but we refused in protest at the abuse we had suffered from the Thai military, which had abducted our people some days ago.

Some time passed by without any news. One morning, staff and representatives from various international organizations such as Human Rights International amassed in front of the refugee camp. There were many other organizations but I could not remember all of them. The guards denied them entry and said that they needed permission from the Thai Interior Ministry. They stood outside the refugee camp the whole morning, trying to get to us. They made appointments to interview us. From that day onwards, the various organizations rostered their staff to visit us every day so that none of us could be forcefully taken away again.

The refugee camp became noisier due to these daily visitors. We also received some donations according to our requests. Still, we remained on alert to resist any attempts by the powerful Thai military to snatch any one of us away.

At this time, a few more new refugees arrived. They described to us the vicious scheme of the Thai army that lied about needing volunteers from the refugee camps to build a fortress against the Khmer Rouge. Instead, such volunteers were taken to log trees in the forest. After all the big trees had been felled, the Thai soldiers gathered them together and started shooting them to silence them forever. The few who survived this ordeal to come here alive had escaped because they became suspicious of the intentions of the Thais who wandered around aimlessly and carried arms that were different from the usual. They fled into the forest where they lost their way for two days. Then they met another group of Thai soldiers patrolling the border. They told these Thai soldiers that they were fleeing the Khmer Rouge and had been brought here.

A few days later, the section chief from one of the international organizations told us that they had found four of our seven youth. They were still searching for the remaining three youngsters. At the same time, I received the happy news that my good friends from *Snuol* Tree Detention Center – Saran and a few others – who had volunteered to go and fight the Khmer Rouge had arrived safely at the refugee camp called Khao I Dang.

Saran related his volunteer stint to me at the end of April 2014. It was in the middle of 1978 when two Thai military chiefs came to *Snuol* Tree Detention Center and took him with others to the Khmer-Thai border to fight against the Khmer Rouge. There were more than ten volunteers in his group. They traveled blindfolded in a jeep the whole morning until they reached a border marker at around eleven in the morning. Their black blindfolds were removed and they descended from the jeep. They were in a quiet forest flooded in many places. A chief made them stand in a row and then ordered them to run straight across that forest. About half an hour later, the volunteers came to a fortress guarded by about thirty Khmer soldiers armed with various weapons. The fortress was nicknamed Banana Plantation. It was headed by Grandfather Saloot, who was assisted by two

Thai soldiers. The newcomers had to practice how to use the various weapons and study different military strategies for one entire week. After that, they were each given an M-16 gun. Their duties were to patrol the border and to ensure that the arrow directing escapees from the Khmer Rouge to this fortress was pointing correctly. The two Thai soldiers flanking the chief would interview the escapees to obtain military intelligence. All the volunteers stayed there about three weeks. Then they were ordered to cut across a very tall forest for one whole day until they came to a deserted village. This village had been abandoned for a long time from the looks of the long grasses and densely-growing young trees. All the volunteers were rostered there periodically. They never encountered any fighting, not even once. However, Saran had heard about armed combat at other places farther away. Their biggest enemy turned out to be malaria. Almost everyone in his group came down with malaria. The chief ordered all of them back to the fortress again. Saran and a few of his friends escaped to Khao I Dang refugee camp because, based on his observations, he analyzed that what they were doing was inconsequential. To the contrary, they were merely serving the CIA's interests to collect information on Kampuchea.

Saran is old now and his spinal problem threatens him frequently. Nonetheless, he continues to serve in medical and artistic charities. He also founded a center to teach the art and science of silk weaving to young Khmer women in Kampong Speu near the Bat Doeng market.

One day, a Catholic priest sought permission from the guards to let me help him arrange the mosquito nets and blankets in his car, which was parked in front of the refugee camp. A guard stood in front of the gate observing us. His car was a family saloon with five doors. He unlocked the back door and left it ajar. Then he pushed my neck down into the car boot with him. I saw that all the things in his car were neatly arranged. I became puzzled what he wanted me to do. Out of the blue, he asked in French, "Why did you do this? Who wrote the letter to the French Embassy?"

I replied in French that it was indeed me.

He continued, "You must leave this place quickly. If not, when the Thais find out that you were the one who had complained to the Embassy, you will die for sure. So, you must secretly ask and note down the names of all the people who want to go to France. Tomorrow I will come and get the names from you."

The Catholic priest then drove off.

I went back into the refugee camp. That day, I walked around, asking those I trusted and registering the names of those interested. The list contained scores of names.

The next day, I gave the list to the Catholic priest when he visited. He swiftly hid it from the Thai guards' sight.

About one week after I delivered the list of names to the Catholic priest, he returned with a representative from the French Embassy. They called out our names individually from the list. There were many more names on the list that I had submitted, but in the end, only twenty-three of us voluntarily chose to leave for France. Many changed their mind as they longed to return to their native village eventually. I took with me Ley, the son of Roeung, who was my sworn younger brother. All twenty-three of us left the refugee camp together.

I was concerned about the rest of the people remaining in the camp. Suddenly, I heard insults and curses from them that stung my ears. I could not fathom why they were angry with us. Then I caught an utterance, "… cowardly group of traitors who abandoned their country…" and realized that they had previously received my word to go home and fight together but now I had broken my promise.

We stayed together in a Bangkok prison for about a week, isolated from the other prisoners. The Catholic priest came to visit us every day. By then, I had found out his name was Father Robert Venet.

Before Roeung's son and I boarded our flight, Father Venet gave me fifty US dollars and a pair of long pants because my only belonging then was a pair of shorts in shreds.

Subsequently, Father Venet helped tremendously to facilitate the reunion with my wife and seven children by arranging for them to come to France within a short time.

Father Venet passed away peacefully from old age in 2013. I send my highest respect and deepest gratitude to his soul now in heaven.

Viva la France

The Air France flight took off from Don Mueang International Airport in Bangkok and headed directly for Paris with all twenty-three of us on board. We reached Charles de Gaulle International Airport near Paris around five in the morning. The weather was chilling to the bone.

Snow floated down, covering the yard of the airport in white. I was very excited to see this strange scenery. I pressed against the glass window of the airport waiting hall. My eyes unexpectedly caught sight of some snowflakes drifting down placidly. The sight lifted my spirit high up into a wide expansive space.

The day before, I was suffering in hell, but today, I had arrived in heaven.

Everything around me was huge and strange. It was not the heaven of my dreams. Instead, it was a man-made heaven. I remembered my French teacher having taught me about France and its political system, history and civilization. France was a major world power and I was now on its territory. What would the French government do with me? Where would they take me to?

Despite my worries, I figured that any place was better than being imprisoned in Thailand. I was drowning in my reverie when someone told us to assemble at another area. I collected myself and headed straight towards the designated place, holding the hand of my adopted son.

At a corner of the hall, there were four men dressed in European-styled clothing, which suggested that they were French. This was the first time that I had seen this fashion style with my own eyes. I had seen such clothes before in French movies, but that was a long time ago, in the 1950s. A pleasant, smiling lady was waiting for us. She was the chief of the French Red Cross and was very friendly. She asked me to help her with the interpretation. She checked our individual identity and handed us a piece of official paper each. After these had been distributed, we waited there for the coach that would transport us from the airport. Suddenly, I heard a voice calling, "Brother!"

I turned around to see who was shouting. All of a sudden, those four men in European-styled clothing ran to embrace me with happiness. I was confused as I did not recognize them. We had not seen each other since the end of 1973 when I had been sent to work in Battambang as punishment for protesting against the government of Son Ngoc Thanh. Moreover, all of them looked different after staying in Europe for a long time.

One instant later, I remembered all of them clearly because they were my close friends. They helped me to change my clothes so that I began to look like them. In addition, they agreed to give me three thousand francs each. Was this not a truly marvelous story that I, who was treated as a beast by the Khmer Rouge ruling over Democratic Kampuchea from 17 April 1975 until 21 April 1978, and thereafter by the Thai prison authorities until 8 December 1978, should suddenly be transformed into a fashionable new man in a sophisticated and civilized country on 9 December 1978?

My four friends who received me at the Charles de Gaulle airport were: Mr. Nev Se, Mr. Pen Vano, Mr.

Kang Ven and Mr. Neou Samau. Mr. Neou Samau passed away in 1980. May his soul rest in eternal peace.

Around seven thirty in the morning, a big bus took us from the airport directly to a center for refugees in Herblay. We would stay here temporarily, pending allocation to different localities in various regions of France. The rooms at the center were clean, neat and attractive. We were given ample meals of French food three times a day.

The center organized all kinds of interesting activities to keep us occupied during our one-month stay there, such as cultural dance performances, movie screenings and health treatments. This one-month waiting period was also to help us acclimatize to the extremely cold winter in France that year. In addition, many kind people donated their old winter clothes to us.

When I was there, I met an old lady named Madame Monique Bellon. I am deeply indebted to her. She helped me and my adopted son tremendously, enabling us to settle in quickly. If not for her help, I would have suffered greatly, but because of her kindness, I adapted quickly to life in France and got to know various French agencies that I could approach for help. I also joined the association for Khmer refugees.

With her assistance, I collected old clothes, tools and instruments to distribute to the Khmer refugees who lacked these things. I did this work by contacting her for many years. Both of us shared a common creed: "We must do it ourselves if we want good results." This motto became our bond of friendship. When she grew old and frail, she left Paris to live in the city of Torques near Deauville. She died there alone peacefully.

After one month at the center, the French authorities split us up and assigned us to various centers in different regions. My adopted son and I were sent to a center named Lagny, not far from Paris. This center provided us with some cash assistance for food and transport. We needed to move around to sign various papers, search for help and visit friends.

I started feeling anxious, unhappy and troubled during the two months I stayed at Lagny. I missed my wife, my children, my mother, my siblings and other beloved friends.

My friend, Nev Se helped me to find work at Bouffemont Hospital where he worked. Through the compassion of the hospital director and the help from my friend who was a very good employee at the hospital, the director allowed me to work as the night nurse. He provided a clean room for me and my adopted son inside the hospital that was near to the residence of my friend, Nev Se and his family. I received a decent salary to support my adopted son and myself adequately.

I shall always remember the mercy and understanding of Dr. Joussaume, Director of Bouffemont hospital; and of my friend, Nev Se and his wife named Yan who treated me like their own brother.

From the day I arrived in France, my immediate obligation that I had resolved to fulfill before leaving Cambodia was to announce to the world the horrific and inhumane acts of the insane and murderous Khmer Rouge ruling Democratic Kampuchea. Thanks to the strong and enthusiastic support from friends and some French associations, I was able to accomplish this mission in France and had plans to broadcast the truth to the other European countries, and eventually the whole world.

On 7 January 1979, a group of Khmer intellectuals with political inclination invited me to a meeting at the Paris home of a Cambodian to seek a common position on the developments in our country. As soon as we had gathered, the house owner received a call from a Reuters correspondent seeking our opinions on the breaking news of the Vietnamese-led victory over Democratic Kampuchea.

All of us were unwilling to embrace this victory. On one hand, we were strongly opposed to the Khmer Rouge. On the other hand, we were suspicious of Vietnam's intentions, as it had in the nineteenth century annexed Cambodia as one of its provinces. We deliberated together to formulate a common position on this latest development. We understood that our country was the victim of a tragic history and we had no choice but to accept the current reality, because "in the water, the crocodile rises above the tiger." We needed to calibrate a nuanced balance between opposing the Khmer Rouge and opposing the Vietnamese army on Khmer territory. This position was not completely satisfactory to us because we were victims of the Khmer Rouge but were now considered spectators. Even though we were no longer living in Cambodia and would not be directly affected, we were highly distressed and tormented. We could not hold back our tears of anguish. My tear ducts burst that day, and could not close tightly since then.

At that time, I often wondered how many Khmers died each day because of this war. Another pressing concern was my family: were my wife, children, mother and siblings alive or dead? If they were still alive, where were they now?

These questions were always on my mind.

I kept myself busy to preserve my sanity. I started an association to create a platform for Khmers to meet each other, as well as for them and interested French thinkers to meet and exchange ideas to resolve the Cambodia problem. We were granted an audience in Paris with our charismatic and highly respected king, Samdech Norodom Sihanouk. We hoped His Majesty would lead a united movement to free our country. We gathered thousands of Khmer refugees to attend this meeting at Baltar House to pay our respect to the royal couple. To our great astonishment, we were informed that His Majesty had left for Changsuwon palace in North Korea for security reasons. We did not understand the king's thinking but we later heard officially that he did not keep the appointment with us because he considered us former republicans. We were deeply disappointed, although we continue to respect him even until today because of his infinite compassion and mercy.

Without the king as our patron, we soldiered on using whatever means we could. We sowed nationalist seeds in the young minds of Khmer children. We organized traditional festivals to preserve our culture. We created a bilingual newsletter in Khmer and French. Our newsletter was very well-received due to the close collaboration between the young and old intellectuals. It presented to readers outside of Cambodia the problems faced by Cambodia and its diaspora. Besides factual reporting, there were also articles for general knowledge; an editorial; and letters from readers expressing their own opinions.

My job was to search for articles from different newspapers and journals and to translate them into Khmer and French. I typed these up using an old typewriter. Then I cut out the text to paste on a page until it was filled up. This process was repeated until all the pages were full. I worked on this doggedly, neglecting my own wellbeing. This work exhausted my energy and personal funds too.

We accepted letters from every political inclination but did not publish propaganda. Our newsletter was an open forum for readers to express their views on the problems facing Cambodia or Cambodians. My work was not limited to the newsletter. I was also elected by both Khmer and French members as director of the Khmer Center in France after the incumbent left to work for the Asian Development Bank in the Philippines. I could not refuse this position because I wanted to ensure that the center's neutral position would be safeguarded.

All these heavy responsibilities took their toll on me physically, emotionally and mentally. I thought that I had lost my country, my wife, my children and my family. What was I continuing to live for?

One day, I broke down and wept uncontrollably because I thought that Vietnam would surely annex Cambodia as one of its provinces. Just then, a heavy hand patted my shoulder. I turned around and saw the younger brother of my former teacher. He was a highly respected doctor of law. He spoke to me gently that our country was like the mystical phoenix that, after living for a very long time, would set itself on fire in the forest. When it has completely burned into ashes, one feather would remain to give birth to a new phoenix, better adapted to the new living conditions it is in. Likewise, Cambodia will exist eternally.

My other important life mission was to search for my family. If something bad should happen to them, I would never be able to erase the remorse and regret I felt for leaving them. I took every opportunity I could to enquire from any new Khmer refugees in Paris and in the suburbs for news of them. One piece of frightening news stunned me: the Thai army had forced tens of thousands of Khmer refugees down Preah Vihear Mountain back into Kampuchea. The Red Cross of Monaco took aerial photographs of this mass exodus and estimated that half of these people died. I sought help to search for my family by putting up notices at the refugee camps along the Khmer-Thai border.

The amazing news that I never dared to imagine I would receive came from a Catholic priest who wrote to me attaching a photo of my family. This letter was hand-delivered to me and conveyed the incredible news that my wife and children had arrived safely at the border. I was over the moon at this overwhelmingly jubilant news. I experienced irregular heartbeats from running around, searching for friends who could help me to bring them to France. One friend assured me that he would help me to do so urgently. However, he did not manage to meet my family. My son Yoopeer saw my public notice seeking their whereabouts stuck on a border post and took it to his mother, who in turn showed it to Father Venet, the French Catholic priest. Father Venet lost no time and immediately wrote a letter to transfer my family to another camp. Not long after this, my whole family left Thailand and arrived in France sometime in October 1980.

I went to fetch them at the Charles de Gaulle airport near Paris. When I saw them at the airport, I rushed up to hug my youngest daughter, who was only two years old then. She pushed me away saying, "Uncle, you are not my father. My father is in Paris."

After hugging her, all of us embraced together tightly with utmost joy in our hearts. I wished for nothing more now that all my children were still alive. My deepest remorse was having had to leave them.

I now had seven children plus one adopted child, making a total of eight mouths to feed. To provide for them was no mean feat. Out of love and pity for the suffering that they had endured, I resolved to put them as top priority to discharge my responsibilities as a husband and a father. I could now stop searching and longing for news of them. Those separated from their loved ones by death would eventually come to terms with the fact, but those isolated from their living loved ones would never reconcile with it till the day they die. I found a new place to accommodate all ten of us and moved out of the room at Bouffemont Hospital.

One of my teachers, a medical doctor, saw my heavy burden and offered to take care of my adopted son as her own. This lightened my load though I still had seven hungry mouths to feed.

Our lives were quiet and peaceful. Our living conditions improved gradually and we were happy. The delightful laughter of my children provided music in our home, which was full of hope.

My wife worked multiple jobs. She was working as a seamstress and took on another supervisory job at a garment factory with more than ten workers. Her work was very exhausting and required her to work very long hours for wages incommensurable with the effort and hours she put in. The children and I helped her out whenever we could.

As for me, I worked at the same place all fifteen years in France. Our income was sufficient and my children did well in school. Some of them even graduated from university.

I will always treasure the precious memories of those fifteen years in France. In France, I acquired the true taste of life. In France, I experienced sophistication, culture and harmony. In France, I understood my rights, liberties and the rule of law (the French have high respect for the law). The French heightened my knowledge, awareness and courage. I have a profound respect and affection for the French, who do not hesitate to stand up and fight. They willingly lend a compassionate hand to the less fortunate, sick or poor, even to complete strangers. It was said that "France is a safe and happy haven" for the disadvantaged in their times of trouble. The French are patriotic and have loved their country through the ages.

An anonymous organization in France gave me fifty thousand francs to sponsor the printing and distribution costs of sending our newsletter out to every corner.

Even though my work exhausted me, I kept at it for the future of my children and grandchildren so that they would enjoy peace, happiness and harmony in an independent country.

At the end of 1987, a rumor spread that Samdech Norodom Sihanouk and His Excellency Hun Sen would soon meet to negotiate. Even though it was an unconfirmed rumor then, it was important for us and some hope arose in us again.

At the beginning of December 1987, the meeting between Samdech Norodom Sihanouk and His Excellency Hun Sen took place. About one month later in January 1988, they met for a second time. After the meetings of these two exalted leaders, I assessed that both sides had started to reconcile. As a private citizen, I have no political ambition. I simply did whatever I could to ensure the independence and continuity of my country. I believed that my work would not result in any further significant outcomes so I took this opportunity to slowly disengage myself from the association producing the newsletter and from the Khmer Center until, in September 1988, I stopped involving myself in Cambodia's political developments completely.

In November 1988, my wife and I had the honor to meet His Excellency Hun Sen in a Paris hotel. I gained much insight from him at this first meeting. I found him a highly intelligent, frank, patriotic man, and an astute strategist. He was forthright and perceptive about the problems in our country. I was deeply impressed by him because notwithstanding his background as a military commander, he had the finesse of a sharp politician.

In October 1989, my wife and I visited Cambodia. The Vietnamese army had voluntarily withdrawn in the previous month.

The International Conference in Paris to discuss the Cambodian issue took place on 23 October 1991 and reached an agreement on the mechanism for reconciliation between the four political parties. The solution was a coalition government with its seat in Phnom Penh and a supreme governing body under the supervision of UNTAC (United Nations Transitional Authority in Cambodia).

However, Cambodians had to wait until 1998 to experience full harmony in their country.

Cambodia would surely rise from its ashes again. Cambodia has life immortal.

This is the photo of my family at a refugee camp
that I received from the Catholic priest.

This photo of my family was taken at another camp which
they had transferred to before their departure for France.
We are forever indebted to Father Venet for his help.

This photo was taken during our first visit to the
Eiffel Tower in Paris. We had left Cambodia with
nothing but the clothes we wore. All the clothes
in the above photo were donated to us.

We took this family portrait in a rented
flat in Bouffemont in France.

In October 1989, my wife and I visited Cambodia for the first time since we left as refugees to live in France. Angkor Wat is in the background.

This photo of all my seven children, teenagers at the time, was taken in our house in Sarcelles.

Epilogue

The Buddha taught that gratitude is the most fundamental virtue of moral conduct.

We are all interrelated and have received benefits from different people in our lives, whether they are our parents, teachers, relatives, friends, neighbors or even the farmers who produce our food. From the just and benevolent rulers of a country, to the myriad people who have extended their sympathetic helping hands to us when we are in need. Sometimes we know our benefactors, but more often, we do not. Each day, countless acts of kindness and charity take place because people want to express solidarity with or sympathy for their fellow human beings in pain so that the latter too can enjoy happiness and have their suffering reduced or removed. Such mutual support creates opportunities for us to give and receive thanks together. This virtuous circle has no beginning and no ending. In short, it is goodness, or humanity.

Every day, we encounter many people we should thank in our lives. How can we reciprocate their kindness?

To repay the kindness of people we know, we can share our wealth or resources with them, according to how much they have helped us or according to our wish. As for our anonymous benefactors, we cannot reciprocate directly but we can pay it forward by modeling the same compassion and empathy on strangers who need our help. That is, we can do good deeds without choosing the recipients, just like those who benefited us despite not knowing us personally. This is one way to repay the kindness of strangers.

From the time I fled from the Snuol Kaong Cooperative on 5 April 1978 until now, I have made a long list of all my benefactors. Even so, this list is not exhaustive. I place on record my heartfelt and deepest appreciation and gratitude to the following people whose good deeds had left indelible imprints on the lives of me and my family:

1. Towkay Soon and his wife, who helped my family to travel from Nimet village to Banteay Neang village, and then to Ta Kong village.

2. The man whose name I do not know at Koub Toich who secretly gave me rice, a pair of pants, porridge and salted goose meat on the night of 12 July 1975.

3. Puk Kim who led me and Hian Lay from Snuol Kaong Cooperative into the forest, without considering his own personal safety. For this, he died one week later in the forest (on 12 April 1978). Hian Lay also passed away around the same time. May their souls rest in peace in paradise.

4. The divine spirits watching over all the forest plants and animals. I believe that I could not have survived sixteen days in the forest without sustenance if not for their divine intervention.

    I also thank the wild animals that made a path for me, whether intentionally or unintentionally, while I was crippled by my injuries; and the mother-and-child pair of wild bovines that provided cover for me to cross the open field.

5. The Thai farmer who took me from the edge of the forest to the Thai army.

6. The Thai doctor and nurse at the Aranya military hospital who attended to my injuries.

7. My friends Saran, Men and Or, who helped me a great deal inside the *Snuol* Tree Detention Center at Aranya in Thailand.

8. Roeung and the youth from the Snuol Kaong mobile unit who helped me a great deal at the Buriram refugee camp in Thailand.

9. Dr. Charles Roy, a Canadian who was most helpful to my work.

10. Father Robert Venet, the French Catholic priest who helped me and my family to go to France.

11. IOM, the organization that sponsored the airfare for me and my family to go to France.

12. The French President Giscard d'Estaing and his government for saving the lives of countless refugees by letting them stay in France.

13. The French President François Mitterrand and his government for saving the lives of countless refugees by letting them stay in France.

14. France and its people who helped and sponsored countless refugees from different countries to give them haven and happiness on French soil.

15. Mr. and Mrs. Nev Se, Mr. and Mrs. Pen Vano, Mr. Kang Ven and Mr. Neou Samau. These four gentlemen received me at the Charles de Gaulle airport when I first arrived in France. They remain my close friends until now. Mr. Neou Samau passed away in 1980. May his soul reside in paradise forever.

16. My friend Ly Taoseng who shared many experiences with me as we suffered together from Thailand to France.

17. Madame Monique Bellon, a true friend who helped me every time I was in France.

18. My teacher, Françoise Cornet, who taught me in the 1960s in Cambodia and who continued to help me when I was in France.

19. The Association for Refugees at Bouffemont in Val D'oise in France.

20. The Association "Coye-la-forêt" under the leadership of Mr. and Mrs. Vernier who

regarded my family as their own. Through this association, I came to know the Beter and Boulay families and both families remain close to my family until today.

21. Dr. Joussaume, the Director of Bouffemont hospital who gave me a job and provided a room for me and my adopted son to stay in. I will always remember his kind support even though he has passed away. May his soul rest in paradise forever.

22. Mr. Beroud, the President of Bouffemont Hospital and his office staff who facilitated the government paperwork for me.

23. Dr. Thevenin, Director of Building B at Bouffemont Hospital. He trained and treated me as equal to my colleagues in our work responsibility and authority.

24. All my colleagues at Bouffemont Hospital for their kindness to me. We shared many good memories together.

25. Mr. and Mrs. Thor Peng Leat, who guaranteed the bank loan that enabled me to buy a house in

Sarcelles. They also sponsored my children's transport fees.

26. All my friends, whether Khmer, French or of other nationalities – too numerous to list here – who provided invaluable help to support me and my family.

27. Samdech Akeak Moha Sena Padey Decho Hun Sen, who changed the course of history and brought progress and development to our country even until today.

Separately, I also wish to thank Samdech Kittiprittbandit Bun Rany and their wonderful children who always help and support my family.

28. Lok Chum Teav Bun Sotha and His Excellency General Tan Panhavuth who always sponsor the major celebrations that I help to organize. They have compassion and always enquire after the health of my family like their own.

29. All relatives of Samdech Akeak Moha Sena Padey Decho and Samdech Kittiprittbandit, who are warm and friendly to my family like their own.

30. All former colleagues working at the Khmer Center and on the newsletter *Srok Khmer* in Paris. We created many good memories together.

31. The souls of my late parents who gave me life and taught me to have empathy and fighting spirit.

32. My late parents-in-law who were exemplary models of graciousness and kindness for their children and grandchildren when they were alive.

33. All relatives and beloved friends, for their affection and encouragement.

34. My wife and children who give me strength, love and happiness. When my children were growing up and needed love and guidance from their father, I could not be there for them. Please forgive Pa.

**May peace and happiness prevail until
my country experiences abundance,
harmony and prosperity!**

Completed in Phnom Penh on 4 May 2014

When peace, social and political stability returned to Cambodia, Dr. Chea returned to his country in the 1990's to volunteer in various charitable works. He taught and trained medical assistants and in 2005 founded a youth center in the remote village of Tramkhna to help poor students have access to food, housing, education... and a family. Dr. Chea and his family have also sought scholarships for the students. Thanks to the generous contributions from various donors, the brigtest students have been able to pursue higher education at university level. Currently there are 80 students living in the center and over one thousand of them have left the place.

Shown are photos of the center:

Printed in the United States
By Bookmasters